I0409101

Disclaimer

The information contained in this book is for general informational purposes only. The contents of this book are not intended to constitute legal, financial, or professional advice. Readers are advised to seek the services of competent professionals in their respective fields if they require specific advice or assistance.

The author and publisher of this book have made reasonable efforts to ensure the accuracy of the information presented. However, they do not warrant or represent that the information provided is current, complete, or error-free. The author and publisher disclaim any and all liability to any person or entity concerning the consequences of any act or omission allegedly arising from the use of the information contained in this book.

This book may contain links to external websites, products, or services. These links are provided for the reader's convenience, and the author and publisher do not endorse, warrant, or guarantee the accuracy, reliability, or legality of any linked external sites, products, or services.

The author and publisher disclaim all liability for any damages, losses, or claims arising out of or in connection with the use of this book or any linked external sites, products, or services.

Introduction

If you're like me, then you want to make enough money, so you don't have to worry about finances. Unless you're one of those lucky few who won millions in the lottery, we will need to find some means of making stable income. Also, no, ChatGPT did not write this book! I did use it to check for spelling and grammar issues though, so if you find any, blame the Chat!

Artificial Intelligence (AI) has emerged as a transformative technology, revolutionizing industries and businesses like never before. This comes in the form of making processes run a lot smoother and easier, such as writing, marketing, emailing, and even generating images and videos just from text. AI is now becoming more accessible for daily use and more user-friendly than it was in previous years; especially for businesses.

AI can benefit small businesses and anyone who wants to make money online. There are now many practical ways to leverage AI to drive growth and efficiency. That is why I wrote this book. To help inform you of the AI tools that can help you make money. Remember, these are tools, and you still need dedication and knowledge to make good income online.

Don't forget: **It Is Possible**

What is Artificial Intelligence (AI)?

Artificial Intelligence refers to the simulation of human intelligence in machines that are programmed to think, learn, and perform tasks that typically require human intervention. AI systems use data and algorithms to analyze information, recognize patterns, and make predictions, enabling them to continuously improve their performance over time. This **technical term** means that we can now use algorithmic computer intelligence to quickly form solutions for our workflow problems. This can include making social media posts, writing email newsletters, blog posts, as well as making video and audio. All can be completed using AI. So how can we use AI in business and make money? There are three common ways to use AI to make money:

- **AI Chatbots**
- **AI-Powered Marketing Tools**
- **AI-powered Customer Service Tools**

Depending on your business, you may need all or some of these tools. For this book, we are going to focus mainly on writing, images, and video generation to make sales and earn revenue.

AI CHATBOTS

AI chatbots are computer programs that are trained to have human-like conversations. They use natural language processing (NLP) to understand and respond to user requests. AI chatbots can be used for a variety of purposes, but for us, they will be used to make money. Some of the more popular chatbots are:

- **Alexa:** Alexa is an AI chatbot developed by Amazon. It is available on Amazon Echo devices, like Echo Dot and Echo Show. Alexa can be used to answer questions, play music, control smart home devices, and set alarms. If you are an Amazon fan you know Alexa.

- **Siri:** Siri is an AI chatbot developed by Apple. It's available on Apple devices iPhones, iPads, and Apple Watches. Siri can be used to answer questions, make calls, send text messages, and control music playback.

- **Google Assistant:** Google Assistant is another AI chatbot developed by Google. It is available on a variety of devices, including Android phones, Google Home devices, and Google Nest devices. Google Assistant can be used to answer questions, play music, control smart home devices, and set alarms.

- **Microsoft Cortana:** Microsoft's virtual assistant that was integrated into Windows 10 and Windows phones. It provides assistance with tasks, scheduling, and searching the web. *Note, Microsoft is phasing out this app in favor of new AI applications.

Even though they are popular chatbots and have their place in the AI business world, we need to talk about the most popular chatbot currently as of this writing, ChatGPT.

ChatGPT

ChatGPT is a chatbot and a type of conversational AI that uses natural language processing (NLP) and machine learning techniques to understand and generate humanlike responses in a very natural way. ChatGPT is based on the GPT-3.5 architecture and developed by OpenAI. It is designed to engage in a wide range of conversations, answer questions, provide information, and write almost anything you ask it to. It can even write in your desired length, format, style, level of detail, and even language. If you asked it to write a health blog post in Spanish, then you would receive that request in a matter of seconds. ChatGPT is trained on a massive dataset of text and code, and it can generate text, translate languages, write different kinds of creative content, and answer your questions.

GPT stands for "Generative Pre-trained Transformer." It is a type of artificial intelligence model designed for natural language processing tasks. GPT models are part of a broader family of machine learning models known as Transformers, which have achieved remarkable success in a wide range of natural language understanding and generation tasks.

Here is the official definition:

Generative: GPT models have the ability to generate human-like text. Given a prompt or context, they can generate coherent and contextually relevant text, making them useful for tasks like text generation, completion, and chatbot development.

Pre-trained: Before fine-tuning for specific tasks, GPT models are pre-trained on a large corpus of text from the internet. This pre-training helps the model learn grammar, syntax, facts, and even some degree of reasoning abilities by predicting the next word in a sentence.

Transformer: GPT is built upon the Transformer architecture, which was introduced in a 2017 paper titled "Attention Is All You Need" by Vaswani et al. The Transformer architecture has revolutionized natural language processing and is known for its parallelization capabilities and effectiveness in handling sequential data, like text.

Currently, the version most widely used is ChatGPT-3.5, which is free. There is also ChatGPT-4, which currently costs $20 a month. OpenAI states that 4.0 is more creative in its responses, can handle more text and requests, and can respond faster during peak times. ChatGPT-3.5 can handle about 2,500 words and ChatGPT-4 can process about 25,000 at a time. If you need bulk text rewritten or grammar checked, then it might be worth giving v4 a look. Also, I've used ChatGPT for quite some time and never had to "wait" for non-peak time or even more than a few seconds.

How to Use ChatGPT

The first thing you need to do is go to: chat.openai.com

You will be met with a welcome screen that looks like this:

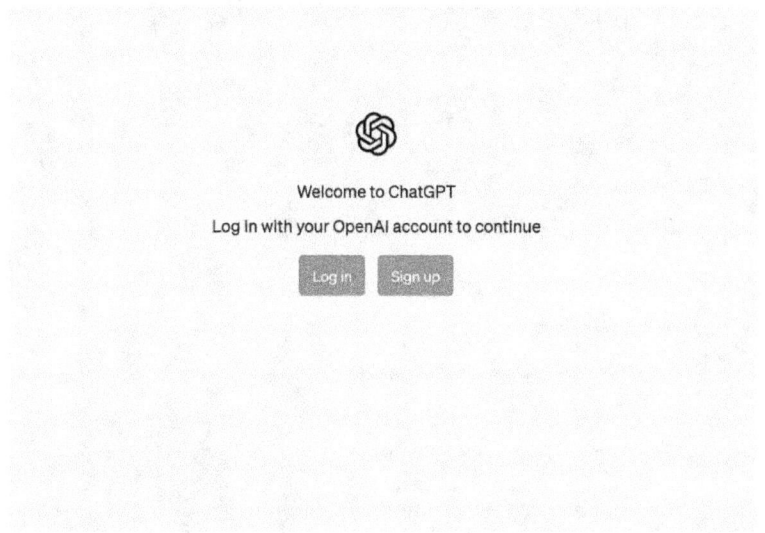

If you don't have an account already, then click sign-up and enter an email address.

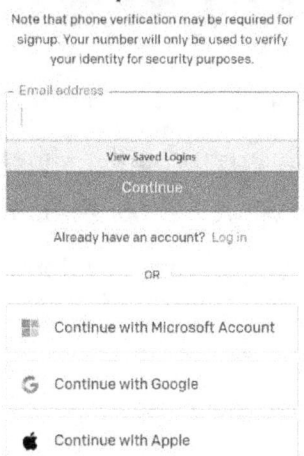

Once that is complete, you will need to fill out a few common questions such as name, birthdate and phone number. You will get a code to your phone (no VOIP) and then you will be in. Pretty simple!

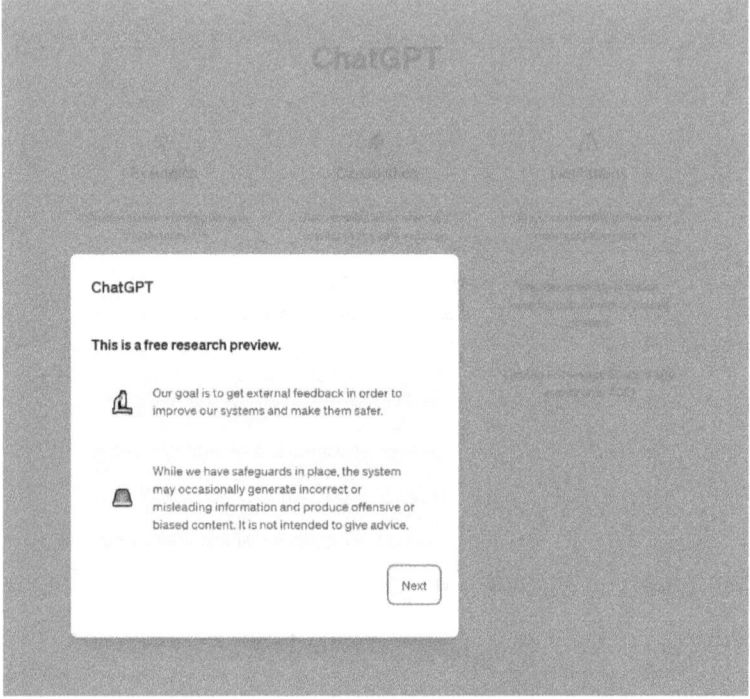

Most likely it will still be a free research mode so there is no cost at all. Be wary of what you write because as the warning says: "Conversations may be reviewed by our AI trainers to improve our systems. Please don't share any sensitive information in your conversations."

ChatGPT is also trained not to respond to "obscene" requests, so if you are interested in working in any adult vertical, then ChatGPT won't be very helpful.

Once everything is set-up, you will be ready to type in some prompts.

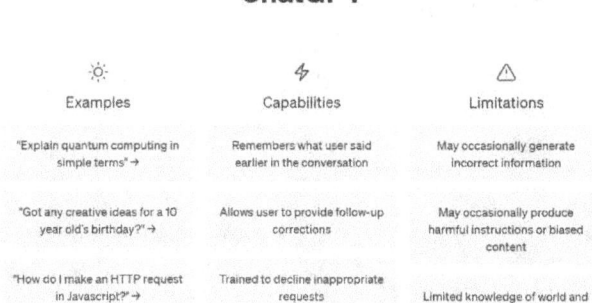

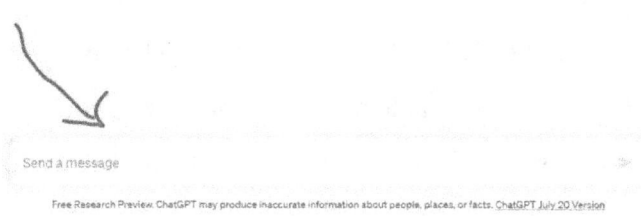

Go down to where it is says "Send a message." This is where you write the prompts. Chat prompts are text messages that serve as a starting point for the language model to generate a relevant response. When you're ready to start chatting, scroll down to the 'Send a message' section. Here's where you'll craft your prompts. The prompt can be a question, a statement, or any other form of information that you want answered.

Let's look at a few examples:

"What is the population of Ireland?"

LB   What is the population of Ireland?

As of my last update in September 2021, the population of Ireland was estimated to be around 4.9 million people. Please note that population figures can change over time due to factors such as birth rates, death rates, and migration. For the most current population data, I recommend checking a reliable source such as the Central Statistics Office (CSO) of Ireland or the United Nations Department of Economic and Social Affairs (UN DESA).

You can see that ChatGPT gives a concise, accurate answer to the question. However, as stated, the last update to the training information model was September 2021. So, if you asked it what are current trends in real estate, it will not be able to answer that question effectively, only give previous stats. But there are other chatbots that are up-to-date. We will check those out soon.

How can we use ChatGPT to make money? It's all in the prompt and how to use them. One great part about prompts is that ChatGPT remembers the previous facts within the same prompt. So, if you asked it "write a blog post about drone cameras" then later on you want more information, in the same prompt you can write "make it more about the video quality." ChatGPT knows what it previously generated and will add new relevant information to the results.

Here are a few ways we can make money with ChatGPT:

- **Creative Content Generation:** Use ChatGPT to assist in creative projects such as stories, music lyrics, artwork, animation, logos, and video scripts. ChatGPT content combined with your editing will produce unique and compelling creations.

- **Write Articles:** You can use ChatGPT to write articles on almost any topic you want. You can then submit the articles to online publications or sell them on a content marketplace as digital products. You can also write articles and turn them into popular videos. You can even sell ChatGPT prompts!

- **Social Media:** ChatGPT can be used to create content for social media such as blog posts, social media posts, and YouTube video scripts. You can then promote this content on social media either through ads or through organic search, in which ChatGPT can write high-ranking keywords for Search Engine Optimization. You can earn money through advertising, views, and subscriptions.

- **Marketing Materials:** You can use ChatGPT to create marketing materials, such as sales pages, email campaigns, and product descriptions. You can then use these materials to promote your products or services and earn money through sales.

- **Freelance Writing:** You can use ChatGPT as a freelance writer and for other businesses. ChatGPT can write articles, blog posts, social media posts, and other types of content. It can even help in technical writing, which you can use to find freelance technical writing work.

Some people have used ChatGPT as a tool to create copy for clients. Some have made thousands on sites such as Upwork or Fiverr by promoting their writing services, such as product page descriptions for their Amazon store; especially for brands that need compelling A+ content. For example, I started in online sales back in 2016 before AI was even popular in marketing vernacular. I sold products on Amazon.com, Walmart.com, and eBay.com, and Wish.com. At one point, I had about 30 products I was selling at one time. I had to write all the product descriptions and bullet points, as well as the SEO, keywords, ad text, and everything else that comes with selling products online. Only a couple of the products had good sell rates, so I hired someone from Upwork to rewrite and optimize the listings that were not performing well. This cost several hundred dollars and took a few weeks. Even then, the job wasn't completely perfect. Had ChatGPT been around, the process would have been a lot faster and cheaper.

One way you can make money is to start an Amazon/Walmart/eBay product description writer and optimization business on freelance work sites. You can make your title -- Amazon Expert | Amazon Listing Optimization | Amazon SEO or something similar and relevant to the platform in which you're going to write. Set your price low to start, then raise it after a few good reviews. Wondering how well ChatGPT works for this? Let's take a look.

I took a popular item on Amazon, its own product of a 6-pack of paper towels. I gave Chat the following prompt and this is the result:

Can you write an Amazon description, with optimized keywords, and make it personable for the following keywords: Amazon Basics 2-Ply Paper Towels, Flex-Sheets, 150 Sheets per Roll, 12 Rolls (2 Packs of 6), White

ChatGPT

Introducing Amazon Basics 2-Ply Paper Towels - Your Versatile Cleaning Companion!

Looking for a reliable and efficient way to tackle spills, messes, and everyday cleaning tasks? Say hello to Amazon Basics 2-Ply Paper Towels - the perfect balance of strength and softness, designed to make your cleaning routine a breeze!

Why Choose Amazon Basics Paper Towels?

❄ **Flex-Sheets Technology**: Each roll is equipped with Flex-Sheets, the innovative feature that lets you use just the right amount of paper towel you need. No more wastage, no more frustration - these towels are designed to be adaptable to all your cleaning needs.

❄ **150 Sheets per Roll**: With a generous 150 sheets per roll, our paper towels will last longer, saving you time and money on frequent replacements. Whether you have a small spill or a big mess to clean up, these towels have got you covered!

❄ **Two Packs of Six Rolls**: We know how essential paper towels are for daily chores, which is why we offer not one but two packs of six rolls each, giving you a total of 12 rolls. So, you can conveniently place them in multiple locations around your home or share with a friend or family member!

❄ **Premium 2-Ply Thickness**: Our paper towels are crafted with a strong 2-ply thickness to ensure durability and absorbency, making them perfect for wiping, drying, and cleaning various surfaces without leaving lint or residue.

❄ **Elegant White Color**: With a classic white color, these paper towels blend seamlessly into any decor, adding a touch of elegance to your kitchen, bathroom, or workspace.

Versatile, Eco-Friendly, and Affordable!

From quick kitchen clean-ups to spills in the garage or office, Amazon Basics 2-Ply Paper Towels are your ultimate cleaning partner. These towels are not only highly effective but also eco-friendly, as they are made from responsibly sourced materials, reducing your carbon footprint while maintaining top-notch performance.

Unleash the Cleaning Power Today!

Experience the convenience and reliability of Amazon Basics Paper Towels for yourself. Join thousands of satisfied customers who have made these towels an integral part of their cleaning routines. Whether you're a busy parent, a student, or a working professional, these paper towels are an indispensable addition to your household.

Stock up on Amazon Basics 2-Ply Paper Towels now and enjoy a hassle-free cleaning experience that doesn't compromise on quality or style. Order yours today and let's tackle those spills together!

As you see, it gave an amazing product description with detailed keywords that are perfect for search queries. It gave attention grabbing headlines for each bullet point, and gave specific details based on just a few words we put in the prompt as well as interesting icons. The only part I would eliminate is *order yours today.* This type of call to action is not usually allowed in Amazon descriptions. Other than that, we have an almost perfect product description in less than a minute. Of course, you will need to go through and add or take away what you think is best, but we have a detailed, marketable product description for free.

Use this for other people's products and you might see your income increase in a relatively short amount of time.

If you sell your own products, you can use a similar prompt to get a product description in a few seconds. If you start your own agency, try not to use 100% ChatGPT. Always put some of your own words in the text. However, it is a viable way to make extra money with very little of your time spent.

In this prompt, I asked ChatGPT to write a bio for a potential copywriting agency for freelance online work. Here is what happened:

I am starting an online copywriting agency to get freelance work. Write a captivating biography for my website that can impress potential clients. The name is AI Writing Room. Make it no more than four paragraphs and write in a fun tone.

ChatGPT

Welcome to the AI Writing Room, where imagination meets innovation and words come alive! I'm thrilled to introduce the wizardry behind this digital wonderland. My name is [Your Name], and I'm the maestro of this linguistic symphony.

Picture a world where creativity flows ceaselessly, and every sentence sparkles like stardust. That's the magic we bring to the table at AI Writing Room. As a seasoned wordsmith and a fervent advocate of all things writing, I embarked on this adventure to create an online copywriting agency like no other. We craft captivating stories that dance in harmony with your brand.

Our journey began with a wild dream: to shatter the mundane and embrace the extraordinary. And oh, have we succeeded! Here at AI Writing Room, we're more than just a team of talented writers; we're a gang of word-warriors ready to conquer the digital realm. From crafting enticing website copy that beckons visitors to explore further, to devising witty social media campaigns that make your competition green with envy, we're armed with creativity, wit, and a splash of humor.

So, whether you're a daring startup seeking to make a splash or an established brand looking to level up your content game, trust us to turn your ideas into linguistic masterpieces. The AI Writing Room is where imagination runs wild, words find their wings, and clients become lifelong friends. Are you ready to join the most adventurous ride in the realm of copywriting? Buckle up, because we're about to take your brand to places it's never been before! Let's embark on this thrilling odyssey together, one word at a time.

Not too bad! It needs a couple of edits, and a little personalization and you have a fully developed biography. If you were to go this path, you could be up and running in under an hour and ready to take on clients.

Note though, even with ChatGPT, you should have some level of writing skills in order to make appropriate edits, but this technique can make you extra money with just a few hours a week. On average, a freelance Amazon product copywriter and optimizer charges $50 an hour. Some can make over $100k by just writing and fixing listings. Remember, the more you know about a subject the better you will do, so setting up an Amazon seller account and making a few dummy products will be choice. This way you will have the backend knowledge. Also, if you have some capital and a product idea, you can use ChatGPT to optimize your own Amazon products.

Let's take a look at another example. Let's say that copywriting and products descriptions aren't for you. Here is another way to use ChatGPT to make money.

Ever search for a popcorn recipe? A simple Google search will bring you hundreds of results. What's on the first page?

A basic recipe search can make you thousands of dollars if applied properly. You can see in the picture above from the website

SimilarWeb.com, simplyrecipes.com brings in over 17million visits every month! Imagine running ads, selling products, or using affiliate marketing on this site. Let's see. I asked ChatGPT how much I can potentially make with 17million visitors a month:

The potential revenue you can generate from a blog website with 17.9 million visitors a month can vary widely depending on several factors, including your niche, monetization strategies, content quality, and audience engagement. Here are some common revenue sources for blogs and a rough estimate of potential earnings:

Display Advertising:

Google AdSense: Earnings can range from $1 to $10 or more per 1,000 pageviews (CPM). Let's assume an average CPM of $5. With 17.9 million visitors, that's roughly 17,900,000 / 1,000 * $5 = **$89,500** per month.

It will obviously take time and hard work to get close to this number, but you can see the potential to make tens of thousands of dollars a month by simply placing ads on your recipe website. This doesn't include affiliate marketing or other revenue sources. A lot of people love cooking and want new and different recipes. That is where ChatGPT comes in. I put a keto recipe prompt in, and this is the result:

Can you write 2 recipes for keto dieters? At least one needs to use romaine lettuce. One needs to use plant-based chicken.

Sure! Here are two keto-friendly recipes, one featuring romaine lettuce and the other using plant-based chicken:

Recipe 1: Keto-Friendly Romaine Lettuce Wraps

Ingredients:

- 1 lb ground turkey or chicken

- 1 tablespoon olive oil

- 2 cloves garlic, minced

- 1/2 onion, finely chopped

- 1/2 red bell pepper, finely chopped

- 1/2 cup diced tomatoes

- 2 tablespoons tamari or coconut aminos

- 1 tablespoon chili paste (adjust to your spice preference)

- 1 teaspoon ground cumin

- Salt and pepper to taste

- Romaine lettuce leaves, washed and dried

- Optional toppings: sliced avocado, chopped cilantro, lime wedges

Instructions:

1. In a large skillet, heat the olive oil over medium heat. Add the minced garlic and chopped onion, sautéing until the onion becomes translucent.

2. Add the ground turkey or chicken to the skillet and cook until browned and cooked through, breaking it apart with a spatula as it cooks.

3. Stir in the diced tomatoes, red bell pepper, tamari (or coconut aminos), chili paste, ground cumin, salt, and pepper. Cook for another 3-5 minutes until the vegetables soften and the flavors combine.

4. Wash and dry the romaine lettuce leaves. Spoon the cooked mixture into the lettuce leaves, creating wraps.

5. Serve the lettuce wraps with optional toppings like sliced avocado, chopped cilantro, and lime wedges for added flavor.

Recipe 2: Keto Plant-Based Chicken Stir-Fry

Ingredients:

- 1 package of plant-based chicken strips (e.g., tempeh, tofu, seitan, or store-bought plant-based chicken)

- 2 tablespoons coconut oil or avocado oil

- 1 red bell pepper, sliced

- 1 cup broccoli florets

- 1 medium zucchini, sliced

- 2 tablespoons tamari or soy sauce

- 1 tablespoon sesame oil

- 1 tablespoon rice vinegar

- 1 tablespoon minced ginger

- 2 cloves garlic, minced

- Sesame seeds for garnish (optional)

- Sliced green onions for garnish (optional)

- Cauliflower rice or zucchini noodles, for serving (optional)

Instructions:

1. In a large skillet or wok, heat the coconut oil or avocado oil over medium-high heat. Add the plant-based chicken strips and cook according to the package instructions until they are lightly browned and heated through. Set aside.

2. In the same skillet, add a bit more oil if needed, then add the sliced red bell pepper, broccoli florets, and sliced zucchini. Stir-fry the vegetables for a few minutes until they are tender-crisp.

3. In a small bowl, whisk together the tamari (or soy sauce), sesame oil, rice vinegar, minced ginger, and minced garlic.

4. Pour the sauce over the vegetables and add the cooked plant-based chicken. Stir everything together until well coated in the sauce and heated through.

5. Optionally, serve the stir-fry over cauliflower rice or zucchini noodles. Garnish with sesame seeds and sliced green onions for added texture and flavor.

Both of these recipes are keto-friendly and packed with delicious flavors while keeping the carb count low. Enjoy!

Amazing! Easy and I'm sure will be delicious. The way we can leverage ChatGPT is to write recipes, lots of them. You can then buy a website domain and make a site using low-cost means such as WordPress. Pick a recipe/food theme for the site that is modern and appealing. Set-up a website with delicious and appealing food and then set-up a once a day automatic blog post. I use Envato Elements because not only do you get unlimited downloads, but you can download WordPress themes, video, and images, all unlimited. You can download a WP theme, add a few stock images related to your recipe, add a few videos to make it varied, and copy and paste recipes to make daily posts. Here is a sample from Envato:

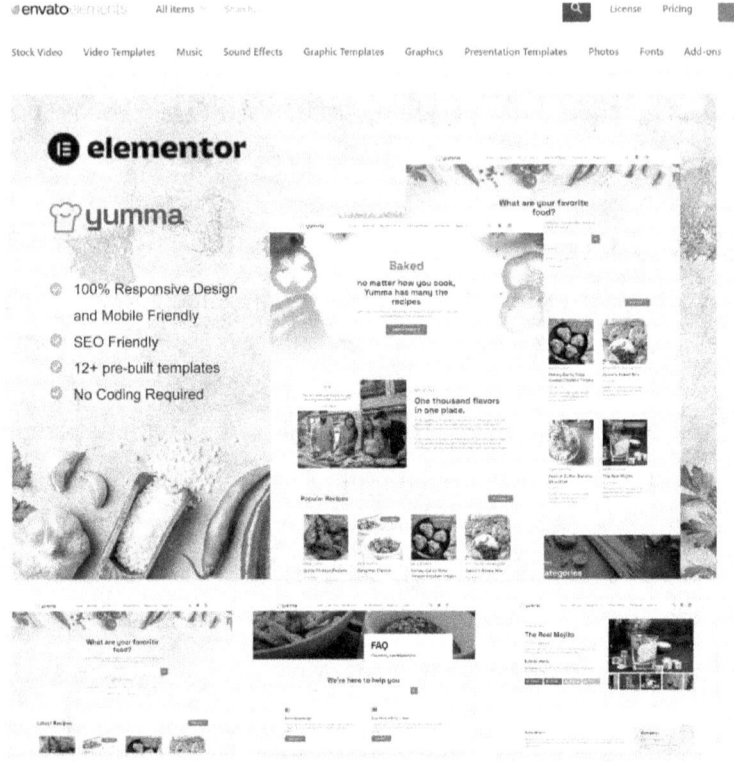

I typed in "recipes" and in the search category, I put WordPress. Several themes came up that you can use for free and make profit. I liked this one because it looks clean and modern. I then typed in "keto cooking" in general search and got this:

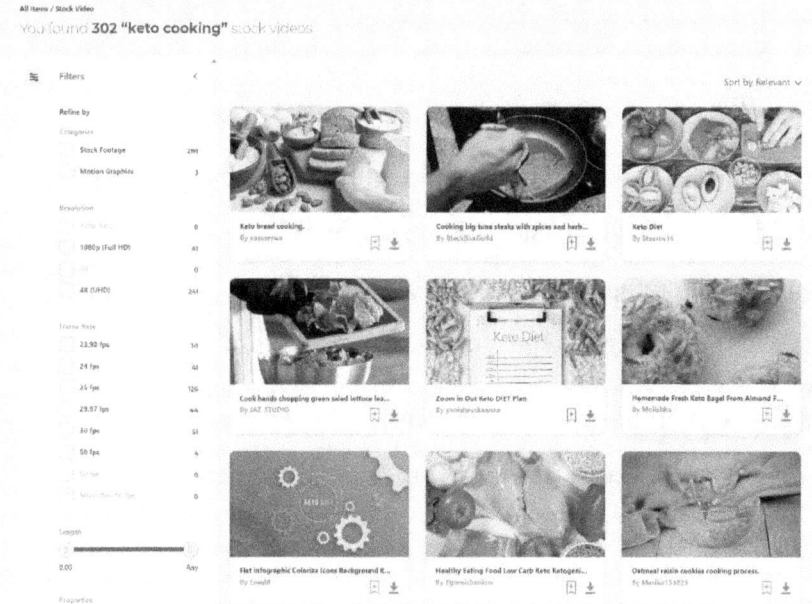

With my recipes, I can add video and images to make the post livelier. Simply add a comment section to get engagement, and make sure you have a star rating system for each recipe, and you have a viable money-making website.

Another great part of ChatGPT is that you can customize it. You can ask for 50 vegetarian recipes without broccoli or great steak recipes for barbeques. Conceivably, you can make months of recipes in just a few hours. You can then ask ChatGPT to make SEO friendly headlines and titles to increase your organic ranking. Once your organic ranking rises, then it's completely possible to rank on the 1st page on Google and get those millions of visits a month. Of course, this will take time and effort, but the **payoff in the long run** can be incredible if you stick to it and are persistent.

Social Media

When it comes to making money online, there is no bigger force than social media. If you can master that, then you will be successful. So how to make engaging social posts? ChatGPT. You don't even have to have ideas; you can ask the program to come up with topics for you.

I asked ChatGPT this:

What are 10 of the most popular topics on YouTube?

ChatGPT

As of my last update in September 2021, the popularity of topics on YouTube can change over time, and new trends may have emerged since then. However, based on the information available up to that point, here are 10 of the most popular topics on YouTube:

1. **Gaming**: This includes gameplay videos, walkthroughs, game reviews, and esports content.

2. **Vlogs**: Personal video blogs where YouTubers share their daily lives, experiences, and thoughts.

3. **Music**: Official music videos, cover songs, and music-related content.

4. **Beauty and Fashion**: Makeup tutorials, fashion hauls, and beauty product reviews.

5. **Cooking and Food**: Recipes, cooking tutorials, and food challenges.

6. **Comedy**: Sketches, stand-up comedy, and humorous content.

7. **Travel**: Vlogs and videos showcasing travel experiences and destinations.

8. **Educational Content**: Tutorials, how-to guides, and informative videos on various subjects.

9. **Tech and Gadgets**: Reviews, unboxings, and tech-related discussions.

10. **Fitness and Health**: Workout routines, health tips, and wellness-related content.

I would pick a topic that you feel closest to and work on that. As you can see, cooking and food are one of the more popular topics. You can use your Envato Elements stock video to assemble a few stock videos and ask ChatGPT to write the recipes for you. Spend a few hours to make 30 thirty videos and schedule 2-4 per week. This will cover about two months of content. By posting regularly, this will help get traction on views and subscribers. You can then link to your WordPress website and vice versa. After a few months and a lot of views, you could have two strong sources of revenue. If things are going well, you can also start selling branded products on your own site, WIX store, or Shopify.

After you built a strong following, your sales should increase as long as you keep making quality content.

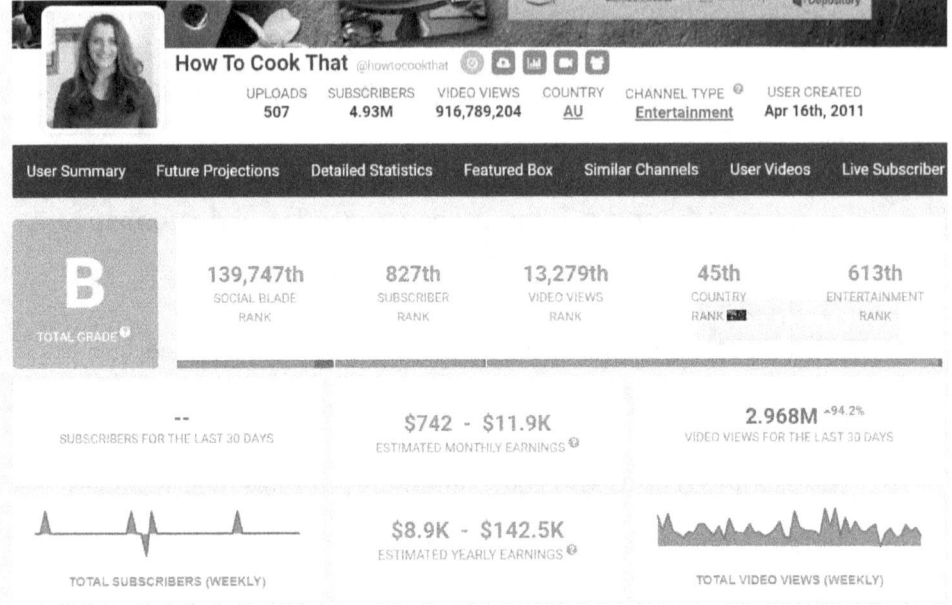

We can see that food is a popular niche. If take a look at one example, *How To Cook That* is a popular food channel that shows how to cook various meals.

The channel has close to 5 million subscribers and over 900 million views. On the high end, the channel makes about $142,000 from just ad revenue. If we were to consider additional income streams like selling merchandise on YouTube, offering products on your website, affiliate marketing, and selling recipe books, it's possible that this channel could generate over $300,000 per year.

As we can see, ChatGPT is the most widely used and powerful chatbot we currently use. Utilize its prompts to engage readers, viewers, and clients. These are all starting points and suggestions to get you thinking. Be creative and choose a niche that is relevant and has the potential to make a lot of revenue. If you are going the freelance writer route, practice making descriptions for a few products before looking for work. Make a few samples that you can post online to show prospective clients your skills. Many new freelance writers make about $6,000 a month if they make it full-time and are good at marketing their services. Remember, the way to make a lot of money is to have multiple income streams. If you can make $6,000 a month using ChatGPT from 3 different sources, that's $18,000 a month with a few hours of work, that you can do anywhere in the world. That is one of the powers of this new AI technology.

Bard AI

Though currently ChatGPT holds the throne as the king of the chatbots, Bard is a close second prince. Even though it's still emerging, Bard is a good, stable alternative to ChatGPT. In my opinion, Bard is very good at creative work such as writing stories, poems, and emails, and even academic research and articles. You can customize the tone similar to ChatGPT, such as conversational, formal, etc. A few facts about Bard include: Bard is a large language model (LLM) chatbot developed by Google AI. It is trained on a massive dataset of text and code, and can generate text, translate languages, write different kinds of creative content, and answer your questions in an informative way. Bard can answer questions in a comprehensive and informative way, even if they are open ended, challenging, or strange and will understand typos in the prompt.

Bard can also generate creative text formats such as poems, code, scripts, musical pieces, email, letters, stories, and much more. Bard can even read the latest lottery ticket numbers and give a calculated response for upcoming numbers based on previous winning numbers. This is something that ChatGPT cannot do since its last update was 2021.

As with ChatGPT, Bard is still under development, and it "may sometimes give inaccurate or inappropriate responses." However, it is learning every day with every use. This is the welcome screen:

Bard can help you debug your lines of source code

Meet Bard, your creative and helpful collaborator, here to supercharge your imagination, boost your productivity, and bring your ideas to life.

Bard is an experiment and may give inaccurate or inappropriate responses. You can help make Bard better by leaving feedback.

Peviously it was only open in a private beta, but now anyone with a Google account (which is everyone) can try Bard. Simply sign in with your Google account and agree to the terms and your in. Once that's complete, you will be in the prompt screen that looks like this:

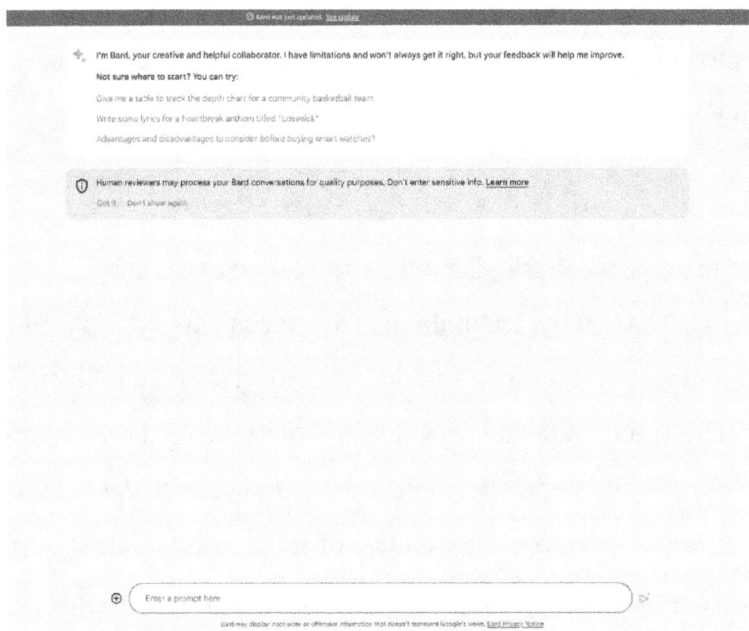

I'm Bard, your creative and helpful collaborator. I have limitations and won't always get it right, but your feedback will help me improve.

Not sure where to start? You can try:

Give me a table to track the depth chart for a community basketball team

Write some lyrics for a heartbreak anthem titled "Lovesick"

Advantages and disadvantages to consider before buying smart watches?

Human reviewers may process your Bard conversations for quality purposes. Don't enter sensitive info. **Learn more**

Got it   Don't show again

Enter a prompt here

Bard may display inaccurate or offensive information that doesn't represent Google's views. Bard Privacy Notice

This is where you will type in your prompts. It is a little prettier than the ChatGPT interface and also has the unique ability to make three different drafts from one prompt. Let's check it out.

Let's put Bard to work and comapre it to ChatGPT. Let's say that you are selling robot vacuum cleaners on Amazon and you have a side site to help build your brand and drive awarness to your product. You will want to make at least 3 blog posts per week. I asked ChatGPT and Bard AI the same question:

Can you write a five-paragraph blog post on robot vacuum cleaners? Make it SEO friendly, and add keywords that are likely to rank high in Google.

ChatGPT

Title: Embracing Efficiency and Cleanliness: The Rise of Robot Vacuum Cleaners

Introduction

In today's fast-paced world, keeping a spotless home can be challenging. Thankfully, technological advancements have paved the way for innovative solutions, and one such marvel is the robot vacuum cleaner. These automated devices have revolutionized the way we clean our homes, offering unparalleled efficiency and convenience. In this blog post, we will explore the wonders of robot vacuum cleaners and how they have become a game-changer for modern households.

1. The Convenience of Robot Vacuum Cleaners

   Robot vacuum cleaners are designed to take the hassle out of household cleaning. With their intelligent programming and advanced sensors, they can effortlessly navigate through obstacles, tight spaces, and various floor types, ensuring a thorough cleaning session without any manual intervention. Busy individuals and working professionals can now rejoice, as these smart machines can be scheduled to clean at specific times, allowing homeowners to return to a spotless abode after a long day at work.

2. Efficiency and Time-Saving Features

   One of the key advantages of robot vacuum cleaners is their efficiency in cleaning. Equipped with powerful suction and cutting-edge technology, they can pick up dust, pet hair, and debris with ease, leaving no corner untouched. Moreover, many models come with automatic charging capabilities, ensuring that they recharge themselves when the battery is low, eliminating the need for constant monitoring and recharging.

3. Customizable Cleaning Modes

   To cater to various cleaning needs, robot vacuum cleaners often offer multiple cleaning modes. From spot cleaning for targeted areas with spills to edge cleaning for thorough wall-to-wall coverage, these devices can be customized to suit specific requirements.

Homeowners can also choose between quiet mode for discreet cleaning or turbo mode for intensive cleaning sessions, making these robots versatile and adaptable.

4. Smart Connectivity and Integration

In the era of smart homes, robot vacuum cleaners have not lagged behind. Many models come with Wi-Fi connectivity, enabling users to control and monitor the cleaning process through their smartphones. Additionally, compatibility with popular voice assistants like Google Assistant and Amazon Alexa allows users to initiate cleaning sessions with simple voice commands, enhancing the overall user experience.

5. Eco-Friendly and Cost-Effective

Beyond their efficiency and convenience, robot vacuum cleaners contribute to a greener planet. These machines consume less energy compared to traditional vacuum cleaners, making them an eco-friendly choice. Additionally, the cost-effectiveness of robot vacuum cleaners becomes evident in the long run, as they require minimal maintenance and save homeowners from investing in expensive disposable bags and filters.

Conclusion

In conclusion, the rise of robot vacuum cleaners has transformed the way we approach household cleaning. With their unparalleled convenience, efficiency, and integration with smart home systems, these devices have earned a permanent place in modern households. Embracing this cutting-edge technology not only saves time and effort but also promotes a cleaner and greener environment. As the demand for these smart cleaning assistants continues to grow, it's safe to say that robot vacuum cleaners are here to stay, enhancing the quality of life for homeowners across the globe.

Here is Bard's result:

Can you write a five-paragraph blog post on robot vacuum cleaners? Make it SEO friendly, and add keywords that are likely to rank high in Google?

Sure, here is a five-paragraph blog post on robot vacuum cleaners:

What is a robot vacuum cleaner?

A robot vacuum cleaner is a small, autonomous robot that cleans your floors. It uses sensors to navigate around your home and vacuum up dirt, dust, and debris. Robot vacuum cleaners are a great way to save time and effort on cleaning, and they can be especially helpful for people with busy schedules or who have difficulty bending or reaching.

Here are some of the benefits of using a robot vacuum cleaner:

- They can save you time and effort on cleaning.

- They can be especially helpful for people with busy schedules or who have difficulty bending or reaching.

- They can help to keep your home clean and free of allergens.

- They can be programmed to clean at specific times, so you don't even have to think about it.

Choosing the right robot vacuum cleaner

There are a few things to keep in mind when choosing a robot vacuum cleaner:

- Size of your home: Robot vacuum cleaners come in a variety of sizes, so you'll need to choose one that's right for the size of your home. If you have a large home, you'll need a robot vacuum cleaner with a longer battery life and more powerful suction.

- Type of flooring: Robot vacuum cleaners work best on hard floors and low-pile carpeting. If you have high-pile carpeting, you'll need a robot vacuum cleaner with more powerful suction.

- Pets: If you have pets, you'll need a robot vacuum cleaner that's designed to pick up pet hair. Some robot vacuum cleaners have special features that help them to avoid pet hair and other debris.

- Budget: Robot vacuum cleaners range in price from a few hundred dollars to a few thousand dollars. You'll need to decide how much you're willing to spend on a robot vacuum cleaner.

Here are some of the best robot vacuum cleaners on the market:

- iRobot Roomba s9+: This robot vacuum cleaner is one of the most popular on the market. It has powerful suction, a long battery life, and it can map your home so that it can clean more efficiently.

- Roborock S7: This robot vacuum cleaner is another great option. It has a self-emptying dock, so you don't have to empty the dustbin as often. It also has a mop attachment, so you can use it to clean your floors.

- Ecovacs Deebot Ozmo T8 AIVI: This robot vacuum cleaner has a built-in camera that allows it to see and avoid obstacles. It also has a voice assistant feature, so you can control it with your voice.

Conclusion

Robot vacuum cleaners are a great way to save time and effort on cleaning. If you're looking for a way to keep your home clean without having to lift a finger, a robot vacuum cleaner is a great option.

Here are some additional keywords that you can include in your blog post to help it rank high in Google:

- robot vacuum cleaner

- best robot vacuum cleaner

- how to choose a robot vacuum cleaner

- robot vacuum cleaner reviews

- robot vacuum cleaner tips

As you can see, both platforms gave a good, detailed blog post, but Bard included examples of other robot vacuum cleaners for sale. This may or not be what you want depending on if you are selling your own product or doing affiliate marketing. One feature we can see is that Bard will give different drafts of the same prompt as seen in this screenshot.

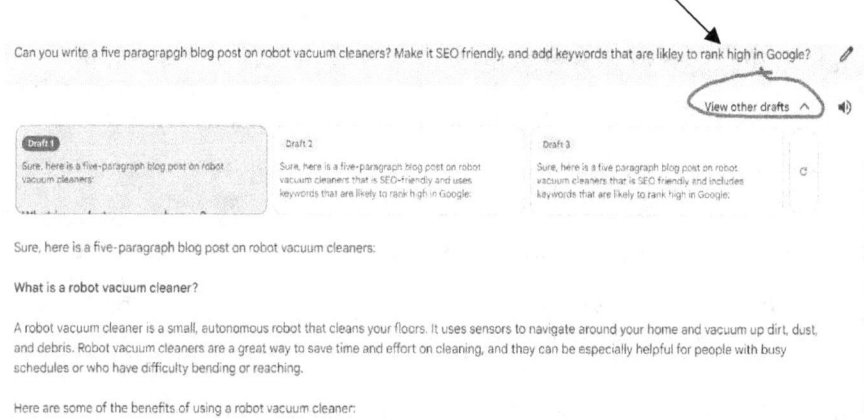

Can you write a five paragrapgh blog post on robot vacuum cleaners? Make it SEO friendly, and add keywords that are likley to rank high in Google?

Whereas ChatGPT gives you one answer with the possibility to regenerate more responses, Bard has three drafts ready for you to choose from.

Let's say that you want to sell short stories online and you need ideas. I asked ChatGPT and Bard the following prompt:

Write a two-paragraph story about a pirate named Neptune the Feared. It should be in the style of Stephen King.

Here is ChatGPT:

In the eerie depths of the Caribbean Sea, where the shadows cast by the full moon danced like skeletal specters on the waves, sailed a dreaded pirate known as Neptune the Feared. Tales of his exploits spread like a creeping fog through every tavern and port, striking fear into the hearts of even the most seasoned sailors. Neptune's ship, the "Kraken's Fury," was a cursed vessel, adorned with barnacles that whispered chilling secrets in the dead of night. Many said it was the vessel itself that whispered to him, guiding Neptune through treacherous waters and granting him the dark power to manipulate the tides.

Rumors abounded that Neptune was more than just a man, that he had struck a dreadful pact with the ancient sea gods, trading his soul for everlasting dominion over the waters. Sailors claimed that his eyes glowed with an otherworldly light, and that the souls of those he defeated were doomed to wander the ocean depths for eternity. None who dared to cross Neptune's path were ever seen again, their fates shrouded in an unspeakable dread that plagued the minds of those who survived. Some even whispered that Neptune had struck a bargain with the legendary Kraken, whose colossal tentacles rose from the depths to claim any ship that dared challenge the "Kraken's Fury." And so, the legend of Neptune the Feared grew darker with each tale, forever etching his name into the nightmares of those who dared to sail the haunted seas.

As Neptune's black sails disappeared into the misty horizon, a collective shudder ran through the sailors watching from the shore. They knew that his thirst for power and the blood of his enemies was insatiable, and that the darkness that engulfed him was an omen of more terror to come. For Neptune the Feared was no ordinary pirate, but a malevolent force bound to the very heart of the ocean, a living nightmare that lurked beneath the tranquil surface, waiting to unleash its wrath upon all who dared to defy the fury of the sea. And so, the legend of Neptune the Feared would continue to echo through the ages, a ghostly reminder of the price one pays when they seek power from the abyss and unleash the terrors that dwell within.

And Bard:

The sea was dark and stormy, the waves crashing against the hull of the ship like thunder. The wind howled like a banshee, and the rain fell in torrents.

In the midst of this chaos, a lone figure stood on the deck. He was tall and broad-shouldered, with a long black beard and a scar that ran down the side of his face. He was Neptune the Feared, the most feared pirate in the Caribbean.

Captain Jack Sparrow was a cunning and resourceful pirate, and he knew that the only way to defeat Neptune was to use his own power against him. Jack had made a deal with the sea goddess Calypso, and she had given him the power to control the sea.

The two ships clashed, and the battle raged for hours. Neptune and Jack fought each other with swords, and the crew of the Black Pearl fought the crew of the Black Pearl.

In the end, it was Jack Sparrow who emerged victorious. He defeated Neptune and took control of the Black Pearl.

Both stories look good and use detailed and vivid imagery. Simply by adding "in the style of Stephen King" the story was written in a horror tone. There are a couple of points in the Bard story that may not seem original, and this is because like most NLP chatbots, it acquires all of its information from billions of sources throughout the internet, so it may occasionally use copyrighted material. In this case, you need to edit and add your own style while keeping the bulk of the AI created material. Use your judgement and don't use anything that may be intellectual property of another person. Some marketers use "black hat" marketing, especially in native advertising (a completely different subject,) but it's always best to stay white hat. You may have seen some marketers use AI to put famous figures in their marketing content. White hat is all of the ethical and legitimate marketing strategies such as SEO building, PPC, social media, etc. White hat is always better. This way, you will create a long-term and sustainable business.

I would suggest using both ChatGPT and Bard when using your prompts. See which you prefer or edit both into a single post. Overall, Bard is a viable, free alternative to ChatGPT and gives fairly reliable and creative responses. Personally, I am currently using 50% ChatGPT and 50% Bard for my daily businesses.

Bing Chat

Now we have Microsoft's answer to Bard and ChatGPT: Bing Chat. Bing Chat is a little different than the other chatbots. For one, it's only accessible in the Edge browser, so you can't use it in Firefox or Chrome. Another is that you do not get a full screen window. As of this writing, it's only available in a sidebar in Edge. If you press the big blue B in the top right corner of the browser, Chat will open.

Once it's open, you have the following screen:

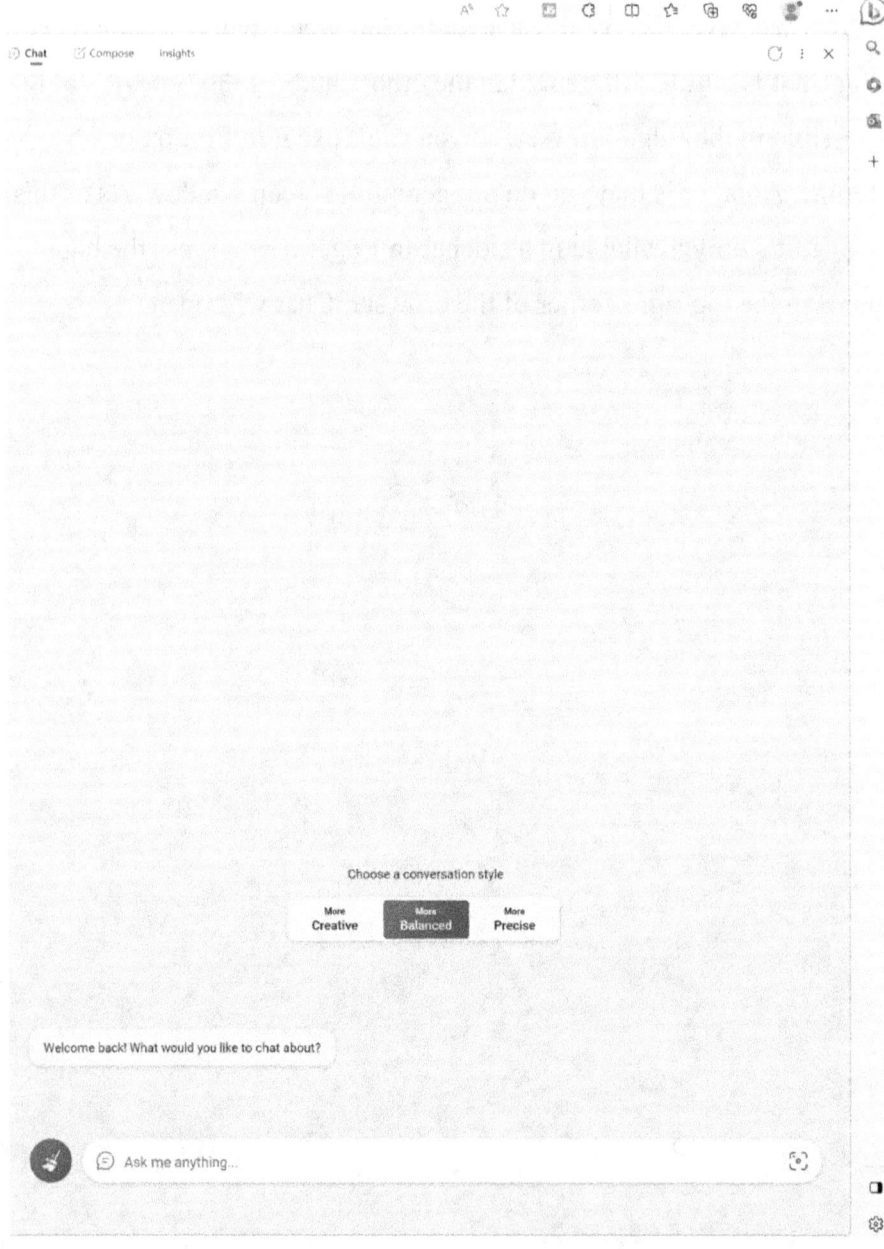

There are three conversation styles to choose from. Depending on your topic, you can use "More Creative" for stories and scripts, "More Balanced" for a good mixture of formality and conversation, and "More Precise" for a more accurate and by the book response.

One of the problems with Bing Chat is that its responses can produce already used data. I asked it to write a product description for a high-powered flashlight I am selling, and it gave me the product description for an already produced product, with the brand name. Of course, this is not what we want since we want original material. I then switched to the more precise option and did receive a more original description, but it is still not the best option right now.

There is also the Compose tab at the top which helps Bing compose work based on your needs. This includes the tone, format, and length.

Write about

synopsis of Pride and Prejudice

0/2000

🖉 Tone

| Professional | Casual | Enthusiastic | Informational | Funny | + |

🖹 Format

Paragraph   Email   Blog post   Ideas

☰ Length

| Short | Medium | Long |

This is a nice feature to use, since we can get customized text based on our target reader.

Bing Chat is built on the OpenAI model, so you may see similar results to ChatGPT. When using Bing Chat, the three options are important in getting an accurate response to your request. For businesses and online marketers, choosing the more precise would be a better choice. If you are selling creative works like books, choose more creative. One thing I like about Bing Chat is that it can give you relevant video links to your question. If you asked it how to fix a Toyota Camry water pump, it will give detailed instructions, as well as links and videos to where you can watch people changing a pump.

Perhaps one day Bing Chat will be a challenge to Bard and ChatGPT, but as of today, it is not a viable challenger in the chatbot battles.

Jasper AI

Another alternative to both ChatGPT and Bard is Jasper AI. Jasper AI is a full AI suite that has multiple tools, not just copywriting. Jasper AI is an AI writing assistant that helps you create high-quality content fast and easily. Like the other chatbots, it can be used to generate blog posts, product descriptions, video scripts, marketing copy, emails, social media posts, and more. One of the major differences between Jasper AI and the other platforms is that Jasper AI can understand context and maintain a consistent brand voice. So, if you prefer a more humorous tone in your writing, Jasper will remember that and make all your subsequent writings humorous in tone without being prompted. If you use ChatGPT to write your blog posts, you may have a different tone in each post. Whereas in Jasper, your tone will be similar throughout each post, making a consistent characteristic. This "brand voice" is good for people who want to run long-term businesses that have a defined feel.

Let's see Jasper in action. If you don't have an account already, you can sign up for a free week trial and use all of the tools for free. Once you have your account ready, you should go to brand voice.

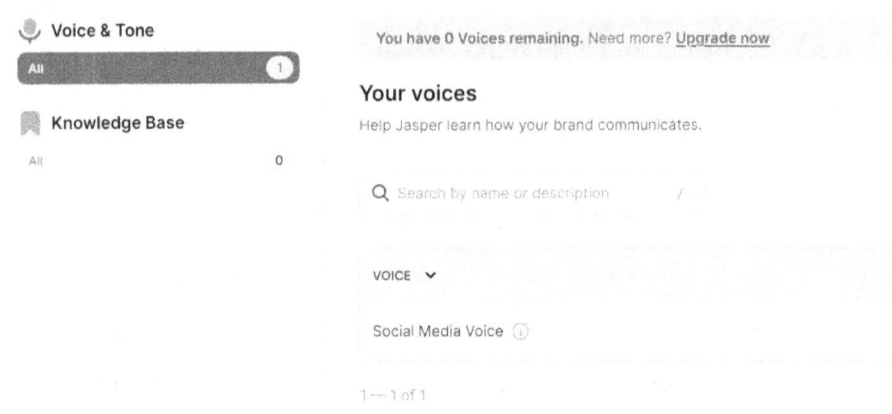

Then either write text or add a URL. If you add a URL, the platform will scour through the website you add. Once it has the information, it will analyze the tone of the writing and make succeeding writing similar in nature. I copied my earlier writing and inputted it into the text prompt box. This is the result:

Modify your tone

Here's what Jasper has learned about your voice from the content provided.

The style guide emphasizes an informative and persuasive tone, using comparison, customization, listing, informative language, cautious disclosure, and positive reinforcement to present Bard as a strong, reliable, and versatile alternative to ChatGPT.

Tell Jasper how you want to rewrite your tone | Rewrite

Name this voice

Social Media Voice

Make it easy to know which voice you're using when writing.

☐ Make default for workspace ⓘ   Save changes

As you can see, it ran a check and discovered the writing tone. This will be the tone for all subsequent scripts written by Jasper.

One point that I really like about Jasper is that it creates original content. According to Jasper's creators, 99.9% of the content will be original. Even if multiple users type in the same prompt, each response will be different. This is a great choice for someone who's looking to make a lot of original content, such as eBooks, and sell them for profit.

Let's try some writing. Head over to Chat in the top left corner of your dashboard. It will ask for your brand voice. You can select the one you created or use a general tone.

+ Create new content...

 Dashboard

Campaigns

Recent content

Your content

Brand voice

Chat

Quick search ⌘K

Favorites

Favorite your most used campaigns,
documents, or templates by selecting
the star icon for easier access ☆.

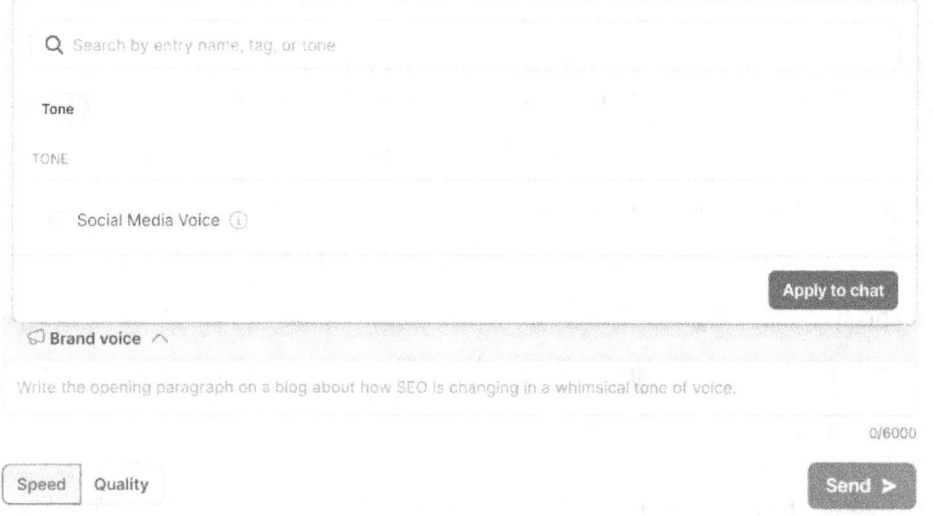

Let's use electric bikes as an example. It seems like almost every bike on the road now is an electric bike. If we check Google Trends, electric bike popularity is higher in the warmer months, but always ranks above 50, which is a good sign.

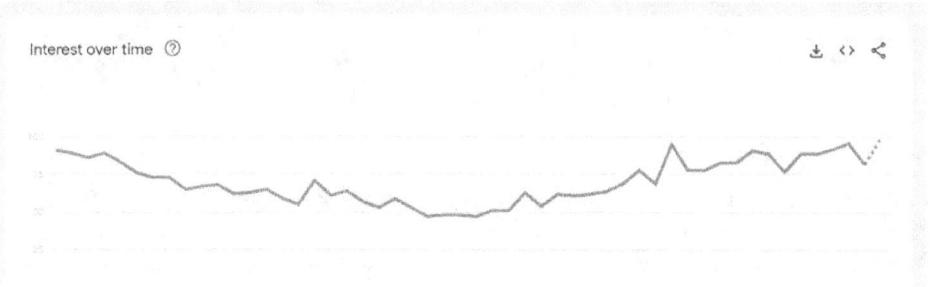

One way you can possibly make a lot of money is to drop-ship electric bikes. This requires very little start-up cost, and you only buy the product when someone makes a purchase, so there's no need to purchase inventory. The only real start-up costs are a website, domain, and maybe some ads. But why would someone buy from you and not someplace else? **Authority.** This comes from consistent posts on your site, social media, and YouTube.

I asked Jasper this question: Can you write a blog post, 2 paragraphs, persuasive and informative tone, the subject is electric bikes?

I asked Jasper this question: **Can you write a blog post, 2 paragraphs, persuasive and informative tone, the subject is electric bikes?**

Electric bikes, or eBikes, have surged in popularity recently and for good reason. They offer a plethora of benefits that traditional bicycles just can't match. For starters, they're fast and flexible, allowing you to increase your average speed and keep pace with faster riders. This makes group rides more enjoyable and less strenuous, especially for those who may not be as physically fit. Moreover, the assisted biking feature reduces the effort needed to pedal, making cycling more accessible to people of all fitness levels[12].

But the advantages of electric bikes extend beyond mere convenience. They also offer significant health benefits. Riding an eBike can improve joint health, aid recovery, and maintain physical activity levels[3]. Additionally, the change in scenery and fresh air that comes with outdoor e-bike exercise can enhance mood, reduce stress, and promote a more restful sleep[4]. And let's not forget the environmental impact - eBikes are far more eco-friendly than gas-powered cars, producing zero pollutants[5]. So why wait? Make the switch to an electric bike today and reap these incredible benefits!

You can see that Jasper gave a blog post of the benefits of eBikes, plus it added footnotes with links.

Footnotes

1. Source: BikeRadar - "The Electric Bike Solution: Transportation for a Sustainable Future" ↵

2. Source: BikeRadar - "Electric Bikes: Clean and Green" ↵ ↵2

These links are important as well. Those links are called backlinks and are important to search engines. We can even ask Jasper to add the site we want to add to the footnote, and it will excavate the site for a relevant article. Also, if you look at the top rankings of Google, they are usually sites that have plenty of backlinks. I use a tool called Ahrefs to check on backlinks: ahrefs.com/backlink-checker

I typed in a popular tech site Tech Radar, and found the following information.

You can see, this site has 24 million active backlinks!

As another example, I typed in Google "new phones." That's all. After the major sites like Amazon and Apple, guess what:

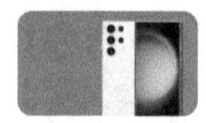

The best phone 2023: top smartphones in the US ...

Jul 11, 2023 — The best phone is the Samsung Galaxy S22 Ultra - but we've also got ... We've already seen some exciting **new phones** in the first half of ...

The Best Phones for 2023

Whether you're looking for an Android smartphone, an iPhone, or a simple feature **phone**, these are our top picks for a variety of budgets across the...

Related searches ⋮

🔍 top 10 best phone in the world 　　🔍 best phone in the world 2023

🔍 t-mobile phones 　　🔍 which is the no 1 phone in world?

🔍 t-mobile customer service

Tech Radar was number 7 on the 1ˢᵗ page of Google. One reason is all of the backlinks. The more backlinks your site has, the higher Google, and other search engines will rank it because they consider your site an **Authority.** Ahrefs also tells the names of the URL's that linked to the root site, so you can get good ideas on the type of website that will link to your respective site.

▾ Source URL

🌐 Press · GitHub
☆ 🔒 **https://github.com/about/press**
`DF` EN

🌐 Daring Fireball
☆ 🔒 **https://daringfireball.net**
`DF` EN

🌐 Future | LinkedIn
☆ 🔒 **https://linkedin.com/company/future-publishing**
`NF` EN

🌐 News & press – Stack Exchange Inc. - Stack Overflow
☆ 🔒 **https://stackoverflow.co/company/press**
`DF` `DEL` EN

🌐 JDN : E-business, FinTech, Big Data, IoT, tendances média, décideurs...
☆ 🔒 **https://journaldunet.com**
`NF` `DEL` FR

🌐 Planet Debian
☆ 🔒 **https://planet.debian.org**
`DF` EN

🌐 Bing AI - Search
☆ 🔒 **https://www.bing.com/search?q=Bing AI&FORM=HDRSC1**
`DF` `DEL` EN

Not all the links all active, but the majority are active daily.
Backlinking is an in-depth subject and perhaps I will write a book about it because it is important in getting organic traffic to your site, but for now let's see how we can utilize AI to increase traffic.

If we look at the first footnote on the previous page, it links to BikeRadar, which is a popular website devoted to bikes. If we check SimiliarWeb, more than 5 million people visit the site every month with an annual revenue of between $15 and $25 million.

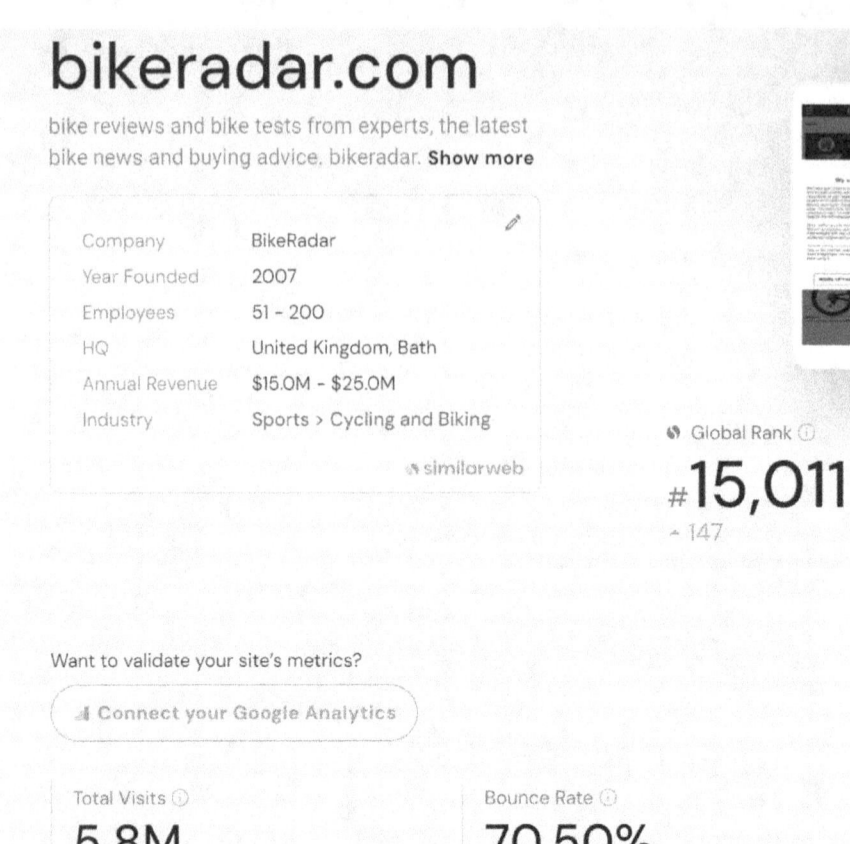

bikeradar.com

bike reviews and bike tests from experts, the latest
bike news and buying advice. bikeradar. **Show more**

Company	BikeRadar
Year Founded	2007
Employees	51 - 200
HQ	United Kingdom, Bath
Annual Revenue	$15.0M - $25.0M
Industry	Sports > Cycling and Biking

similarweb

Global Rank

#15,011

147

Want to validate your site's metrics?

Connect your Google Analytics

Total Visits

5.8M

Bounce Rate

70.50%

If you ever go to bikeradar.com, you will see it is a very plain site, not
too fancy and with a lot of ads and forwarding clicks. It's mostly blog
posts and reviews. This is most likely how they make the bulk of their
revenue: ads and affiliate marketing. If you write a blog post review on
a new bike, and have an affiliate link to the product, you will make a
commission if they purchase it. If you have 6 million people visiting
your site every month, most likely you will have hundreds if not

thousands of sales per month. This is the same for ads. The more people who visit your site, the bigger the chance of someone clicking an ad. The good thing about ads is that the visitor just needs to click on it for you to receive compensation, they don't necessarily need to buy.

We can use Jasper to help increase your website backlinks by writing high-quality, original posts. When you write consistent quality posts, you can link them on your Facebook page. People who read and like your posts will share with friends. Often, other websites "crawl" the internet for relatable content to their own site. If they pick up your content, and it is similar to theirs, they might post some of you blog or products and link back to you, hence backlinks.

Let's keep using electric bikes as an example. Another way to get more links is for you to use Jasper AI to write a blog post, then you can contact one of the writing staff of the site and ask if they will accept a guest contribution. If accepted, your Jasper article will be posted on their website, which can potentially mean millions of people can read it. What is equally important is you will get a contributor credit and a link back to your site. This means more authority, more visits, and more money.

Google considers it a vote of confidence when sites link to other sites that are high-quality. Let's say you have a dropshipping site. It could mean your dropshipping site might rank on the first page of Google just by writing quality posts from Jasper and getting links from other sites. Without any paid ads, all organic.

Another amenity Jasper AI has is the ability to enhance your prompt.

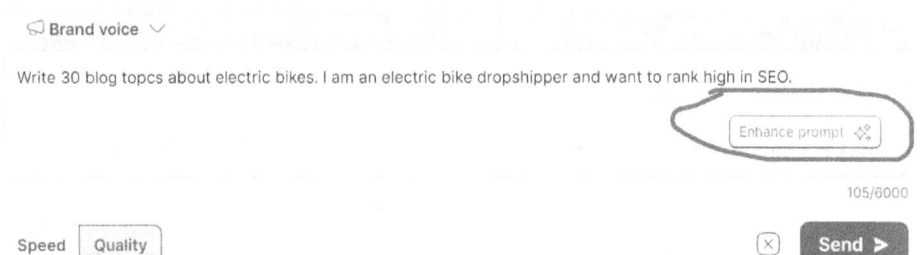

In this one, I wrote: *30 blog topics about electric bikes. I am an electric bike dropshipper and want to rank high in SEO.*

After clicking Enhance Prompt, Jasper came up with this: "act as a content writer. Create a list of 30 potential blog topics to promote a dropshipping business of electric bikes. Focus on providing comprehensive and engaging content for your readers. Consider targeting your articles to a specific audience, such as bicycle enthusiasts or commuters. Use relevant keywords and incorporate topics that will appeal to both electric bike enthusiasts and casual riders alike. Potential article topics may include highlighting popular models, best practices for battery charging, maintenance and safety tips, comparison guides, etc. Keep your audience informed about the latest electric bike technology and road regulations while keeping your writing engaging and entertaining."

As you can see, this prompt is much more detailed and is something that ChaptGPT and Bard do not have. Jasper enhanced the prompt to get a much more detailed response, which will ultimately lead to more readers.

Here is the result:

1. "Top 10 Electric Bikes for the Modern Commuter"

2. "Maximizing Your Battery Life: Tips and Tricks for Electric Bike Owners"

3. "Why Electric Bikes are Changing the Game for Urban Commuters"

4. "A Complete Guide to Choosing Your First Electric Bike"

5. "Electric Bike vs Traditional Bike: A Comprehensive Comparison"

6. "The Future of Commuting: The Rise of Electric Bikes"

7. "Demystifying Dropshipping: Your Guide to Starting an Electric Bike Business"

8. "How to Maintain Your Electric Bike for Long-Term Use"

9. "Best Practices for Safe Riding on Your Electric Bike"

10. "The Top 5 Electric Bike Models for Off-Road Adventure"

11. "Understanding the Technology Behind Electric Bikes"

12. "Exploring the Environmental Benefits of Electric Bikes"

13. "How Electric Bikes are Revolutionizing Fitness Routines"

14. "Increase Your Profits with an Electric Bike Dropshipping Business"

15. "Navigating Road Regulations for Electric Bikes"

16. "The Role of Electric Bikes in Sustainable Urban Planning"

17. "How to Market Your Electric Bike Dropshipping Business"

18. "Why Electric Bikes are the Perfect Solution for Busy City Dwellers"

19. "The Impact of Electric Bikes on Reducing Carbon Footprint"

20. "Electric Bike Accessories Every Rider Should Have"

21. "Unveiling the Cost-Efficiency of Electric Bikes"

22. "Why Electric Bikes are an Excellent Investment for the Future"

23. "Boost Your Health: The Fitness Benefits of Riding an Electric Bike"

24. "Exploring the Best Routes for Electric Bike Riders"

25. "Electric Bikes: Combining Speed, Efficiency, and Fun"

26. "Rider Stories: Inspiring Experiences from Electric Bike Enthusiasts"

27. "The Evolution of Electric Bikes: A Look at the Past, Present, and Future"

28. "Transitioning to Electric Bikes: What New Riders Need to Know"

29. "How to Choose the Right Electric Bike for Your Lifestyle"

30. "The Pros and Cons of Starting an Electric Bike Dropshipping Business"

Jasper came up with a month of topics in about 10 seconds. I can then go in and ask it to write each post and schedule it to post on the day I choose. All you have to do is either ask it "write (then the topic title)" or type: expand/(topic title).

I can also ask Jasper to write product descriptions based on the URL of the product. If you dropship, just copy and paste the product link from the supplier in Jasper and it will write a detailed product description for you to add to your product page.

I got this description after putting a product link from AliExpress in the prompt box and asking it to write a detailed product description for my e-commerce store:

"...a revolutionary product in the world of adult biking. It comes equipped with a powerful 350W Motor that can peak up to 500W, providing robust power and speed for your daily commutes or off-road adventures. This bike is an amalgamation of style and comfort, featuring a sleek design and an air saddle for a smooth and comfortable ride.

In summary, the Electric Bike is a top-tier choice for any adult looking to upgrade their biking experience. Its blend of power, comfort, and affordability makes it a standout option in the electric bike market."

Using product URLs is a quick and easy way to generate and optimize product listings and is something that Bard and ChatGPT are yet to incorporate because they cannot recognize external links. If you have a dropship business, this can save you a lot of time, since you can copy and paste the supplier's links in bulk and get original and detailed product descriptions.

Jasper has dozens of templates to choose from, which can be used for everything from **Amazon product pages** with bullet points to YouTube topic ideas. It's definitely the recommended tool if you want to run a full-time e-commerce business.

Jasper Art

Another useful tool that Jasper employs is Jasper AI art. If you go to Your Content in the dashboard, this page will show up:

Your content

This content will be only visible to you. Any content created by you that is not within a specific campaign will show up here.

📄 + Blank document	🔲 + New from template	🖼 + New art
Start from scratch with a blank document.	Create content using templates and workflows.	Generate endless types of imagery for any use case.

Click New Art and there will be a few options to give prompts. So, continuing with our electric bike store, I wrote a prompt and Jasper expanded and filled it in with a few suggestions.

Art

Free form   Templates

Describe what you want to create

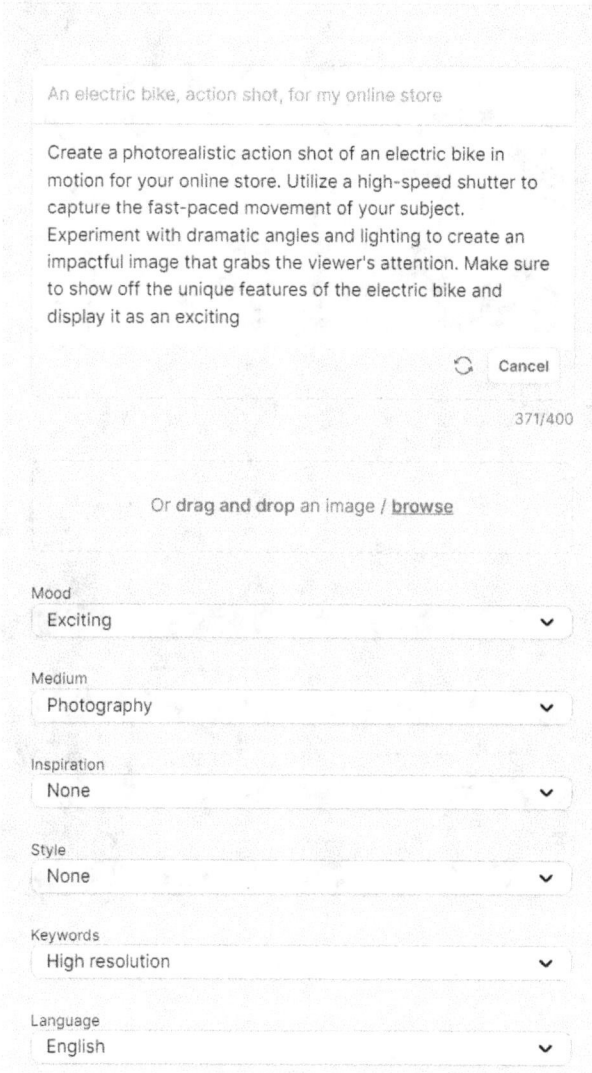

An electric bike, action shot, for my online store

Create a photorealistic action shot of an electric bike in motion for your online store. Utilize a high-speed shutter to capture the fast-paced movement of your subject. Experiment with dramatic angles and lighting to create an impactful image that grabs the viewer's attention. Make sure to show off the unique features of the electric bike and display it as an exciting

Cancel

371/400

Or **drag and drop** an image / **browse**

Mood
Exciting

Medium
Photography

Inspiration
None

Style
None

Keywords
High resolution

Language
English

Here is the result:

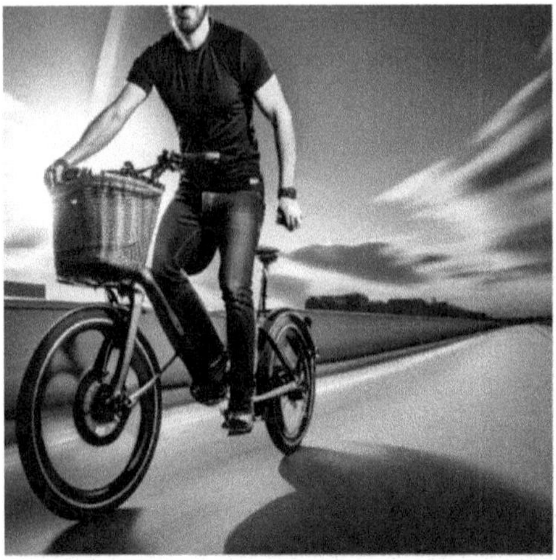
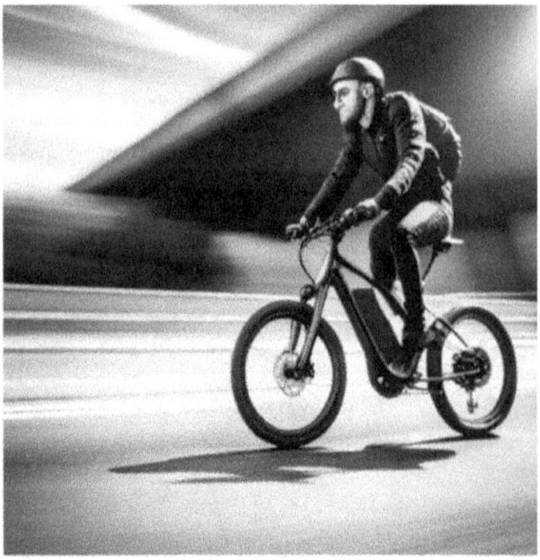
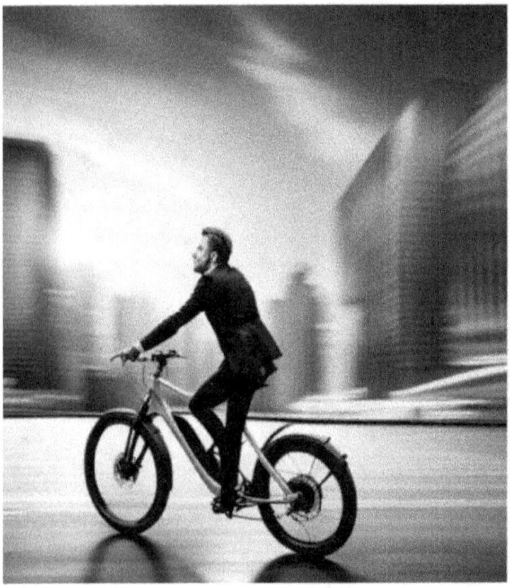
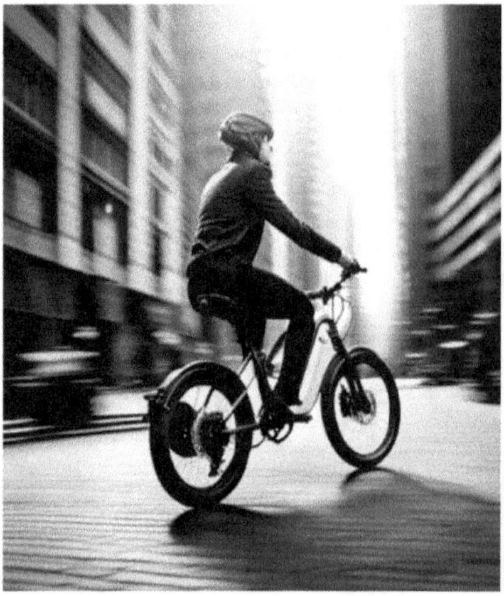

We have a few good options to choose from. We will need to crop out some of the facial features, but overall, these are highly detailed photos we can use for our blog posts or YouTube video thumbnails.

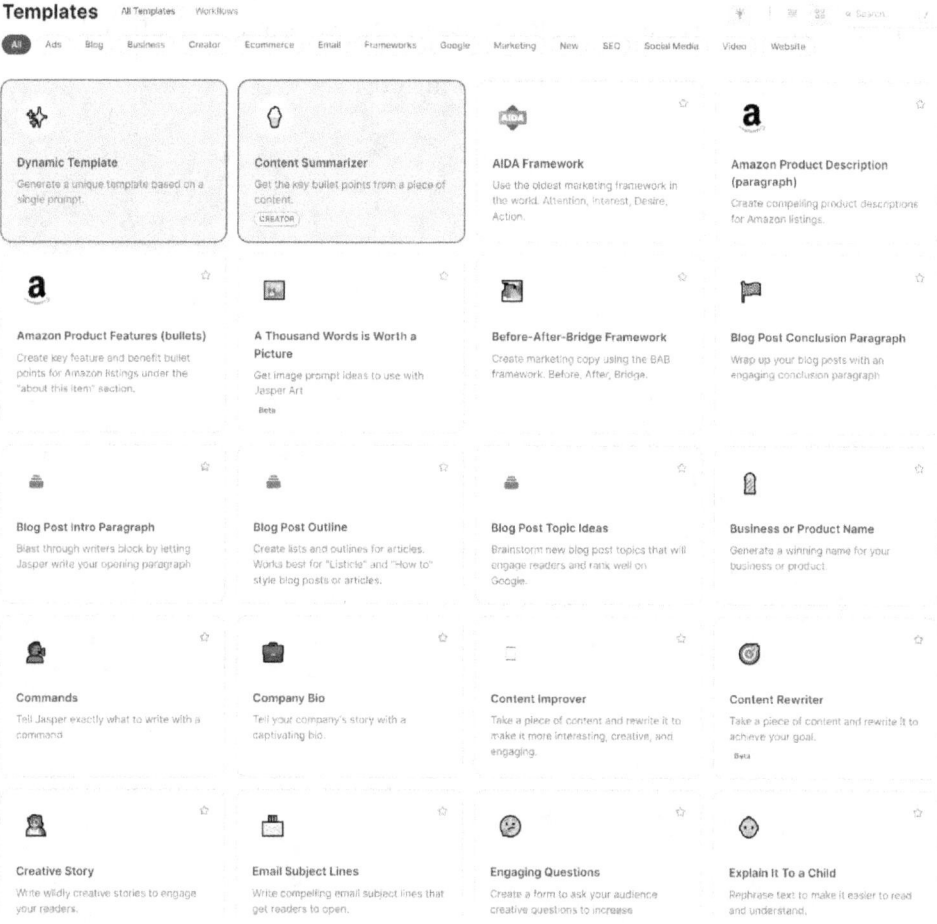

Jasper AI has dozens of templates to use including real estate listing description and optimization, personal bio creator, creative story maker, landing page maker and many more. If you are dedicated to making money online and have a solid business idea, Jasper is a fantastic all-in-one suite of tools to get you into production. It's not free like the other tools, but it does have a trial. If you try it out, use it thoroughly and make sure you have a good idea of what you want to accomplish. If used efficiently, it can be well worth the cost.

AI IMAGE GENERATION

Now that we checked out chatbots for writing, it's time to take a look at visuals. Marketing and making money online are multifaceted ventures. You need persuasive text, compelling images, and intriguing video. What's the first thing you notice when you search for products on Amazon? The thumbnail picture.

It's the same thing when searching for a new car. We look at how well it looks then discover more about the product. If you see a beat up car that's dented with chipped paint, most likely you won't research further, even if it does perform well. Poor images will mean your product will be passed over, even if it's a great product. This is where AI image generation comes into play. We can use stock photos from Envato Elements, but sometimes we will need custom photos that aren't in the stock library. Today, we can create photos from simple text prompts. All you have to do is type in a description of what you want, and the platform will use its algorithm and GPU to generate the resulting image. Let's look at the more popular image generation platforms.

Midjourney AI

Midjourney AI is a generative artificial intelligence program which generates images from natural language descriptions, aka prompts. Midjourney AI uses knowledge of the world and its training data to generate images that match your text prompt. Images can be upscaled and varied. You can also input the exact aspect ratio and even the resolution. This is good for us since we can generate images for different uses such as thumbnails, book cover art, and Instagram posts.

How we can use it to make money with Midjourney is through its ability to create custom, original photos. Let's take a look at it.

Head over to midjourney.com and you will get this funky-looking homepage.

Click Join Beta at the bottom of the screen, then go through the sign-up process. Midjourney is run on a Discord server, so if you have an account, you can sign in, otherwise you can create a new account. Once you finish setting up, click the boat to the left. This will take you to the main server. After that, go to one of the newbie servers.

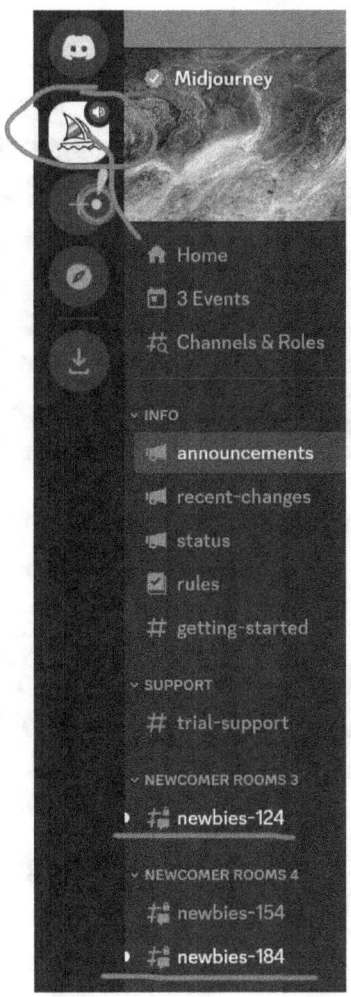

Once you're in the server, you will see a constantly changing number of pictures. These are all user generated images. Since it's a public server, everyone's images will be public unless you pay for a private server membership. Once you are in the server, you can start creating images. All image prompts must first start with the following command: /imagine

After that we can start creating:

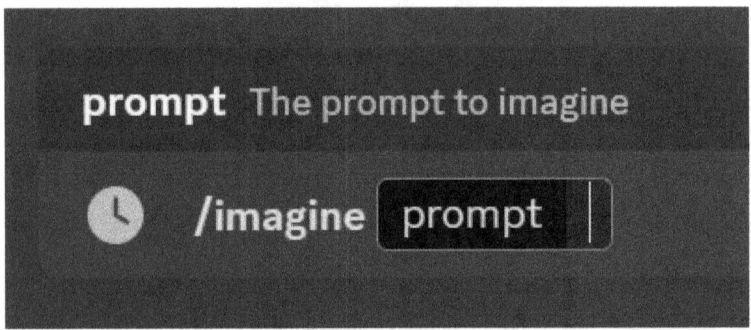

Let's try something simple. Let's try the electric bike image. I wrote this prompt:

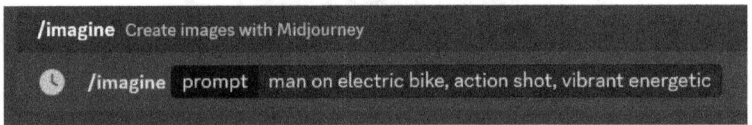

Midjourney automatically gives four options to choose from. They can vary depending on the parameters you set. I got a few good shots, but I really like the third one.

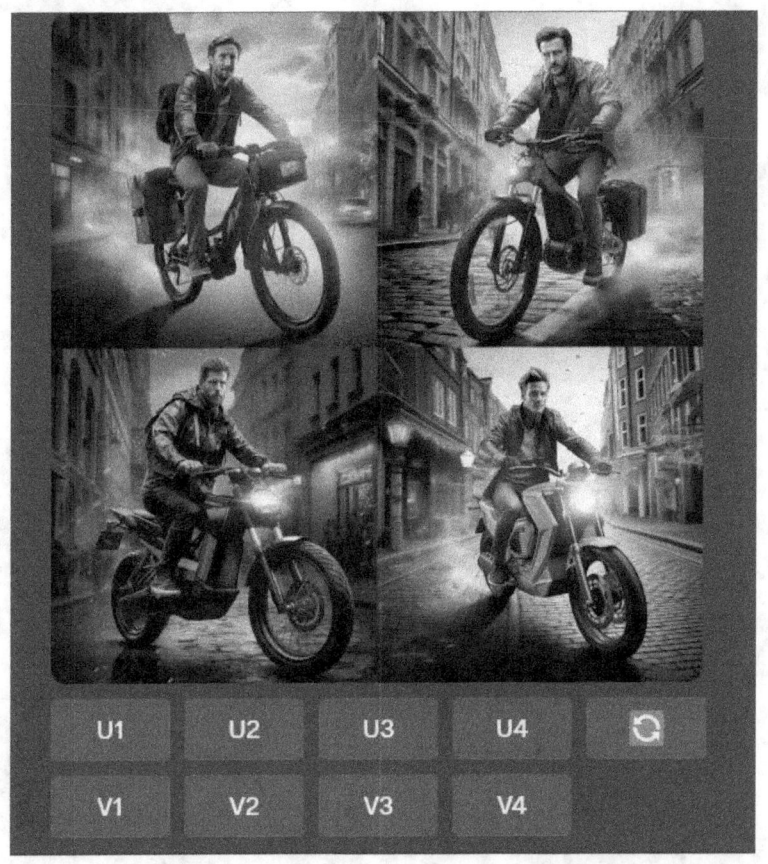

In this case, I can click U3 to upscale the 3rd image. I upscaled it and this is the final shot:

That's a pretty good action shot. The detail is intense, and it has an excellent angle for a promo shot. If I sold electric bikes, I would definitely use this image in my ads and/or posts. Another nice feature in Midjourney is that you can vary the images. If we look at the following image:

U1	U2	U3	U4	⟳
V1	V2	V3	V4	

The v1, v2, v3, v4 mean variation. Our picture was image 3, so if I clicked v3, there will be new variations based on the 3rd image. If I clicked the two arrows that are circling, then all four images would change based on the original parameters. Let's see what developed:

We can see that all of the variation images have the same theme, but all of them changed in small parts. The same main features remain, but there are slight differences.

Instead of typing in the prompt: /imagine, here are a few of the most common prompts:

/settings, this will bring you into the settings menu. You can change the options such as the model version (5.2 as of this writing), stylize mode, which have low stylize that gives less details and very high, which will have the highest level of details — high and low variation, which is used for when we remix the images — according to the image number v1, v2, v3, v4 button or if you use the two arrow all variation button – selecting low variation will give slight changes to the images and high variation will give almost new details to all images but still have the same foundation prompt. There is also relax and fast mode. Relax is used for normal image processing and is slower to generate an image, and Fast makes the image processing speed much quicker. Relax takes longer since the job is queued in the public server, fast takes less than a minute but you need a paid account. At this time, the prices started around $12 a month.

Two more tips we need to check are Raw mode and AR which stands for aspect ratio. Raw mode changes the style and the detail of the images. In these images, I unchecked Raw mode:

In these, I had Raw mode checked:

Both used the same prompt: /imagine electric bike, promotional ad, advertising electric bike, man on bike, exceptional details, photorealism --s 750

Both sets of images have exquisite details and the vibrance is strong and bright. The only major difference I see is that the Raw mode gives slightly more details and deeper color. Depending on the product you are selling, try turning raw mode on and off to check which style you like the most.

Aspect ratio is another way we can change the image. We can use the affix --ar at the end of the prompt, then we can set the aspect ratio we need. We always put -- at the end of the prompt to tell Midjourney that we are using a new parameter. We can change the aspect ratio depending on the needs. Here are the most common types of aspect ratio's that Midjourney uses.

--ar1:1 Default aspect ratio.

--ar5:4 Common for picture frames and prints

--ar3:2 Good for print photography

--ar7:4 Good for HD widescreens and YouTube thumbnails

In the next image, I used the prompt:

vibrant electric bike for advertisement--ar7:4--s750

For these images, I used the aspect ratio 7:4 which is good for YouTube thumbnails. It's basically a 16x9 ratio. If you are writing posts or need to create images for a book, then you will want to use different and specific aspect ratios.

Also, the --s parameter stands for stylization. It controls how much Midjourney will apply its style to the generated image. A higher --s value will result in a more stylized image, while a lower --s value will result in a more realistic image. The default value is 100. You can go into settings and change this, or you can add the parameter to the prompt. If you want to create more realistic images, decrease the --s value. For example, a value of 50 will result in a more realistic image compared to a style of 100.

You can also use the --s parameter to create a specific style of image. For example, if you want to create an image that has a painterly style, you can set the --s value to a high value, such as 200.

Here are some examples of how to use the --s parameter:

--s 100 = Maximum stylization

--s 50 = More realistic image

--s 200 = Painterly style

Experiment and see which settings you like the most. If you are going to generate a lot of images, think about paying for a month of the paid account so you can use the Fast setting. You can get at least 3x more images generated in the same amount of time.

In addition to using Midjourney for marketing images, you can also generate images and sell them on stock sites such as Adobe Stock and Shutterstock. If using Adobe, go all the way to the bottom and click Sell Images.

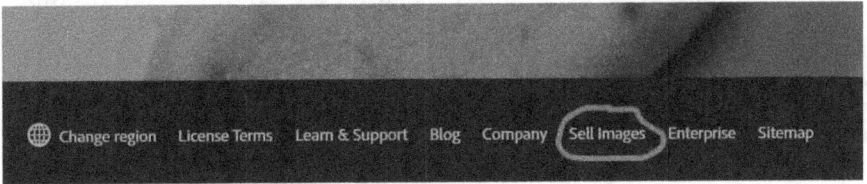

Create an account, then upload your images. You select the category and write a description. The same process goes for Shutterstock, iStockphoto, Creative Market and more. These sites recently opened to accept AI stock art, so it's not a crowded space right now. What I do is search for popular images, then create similar images using AI. You get a commission every time someone downloads your image. Creative Market gives one of the higher splits at 60% commission of the final price. Most likely you won't make a ton of money using this method, but if you can make a few hundred dollars a month more just by making AI images, it's definitely worth the minimal time and effort.

Another avenue you can use is to sell your images as digital art, book covers, characters, or prints.

Remember how we thought about starting a freelance copywriting business on Fiverr or Upwork? We can do the same for art. You can make AI book covers or logos. Since the client usually has a look in mind, you can use this as a prompt to create the image.

Let's say a client runs a wine business. They are looking for a new logo. You can go to Midjourney and create a logo in seconds. I used the following prompt: wine glass, classy, sparkle on top of glass, light blue background, logo vector logo--s 750

Here is the result:

wine glass, classy, sparkle on top of glass, light blue background, logo vector logo --s 750

We have four great images to start with. We can customize and revise until we get the desired image, but this is a great start. If you want to have similar characteristics throughout your variations, you can use the Upload feature to upload an image.

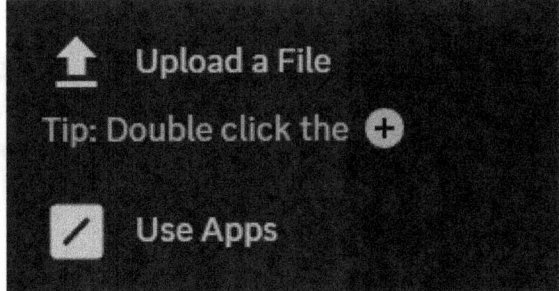

You'll see a + next to where you type in your prompt. Click it, then Upload the file. Upload the main source photo and hit Enter twice. Then click on the image, and right click and copy the Image Adress. This will be a URL. Then do a normal /imagine - then paste the image URL. At the end of the URL, add the details you want. For the wine glass, I uploaded the photo, copied and pasted the link, then added "empty wine glass." This tells Midjourney to use the data from the uploaded image and add new details, which in this case, is empty glass.

This is the result:

You can see that the original image was used, plus we got new variations of an empty glass. You can use this method to create consistent images over time. You can use this same method to create book covers for clients. Combine the two jobs to maximize your income potential.

The average logo and book cover designer charges $35 an hour on Upwork at around 5-10 hours per project. The more complex the logo, the more you can up your work hours. Many freelancers make a few thousand a month just with logo creation. Some of the more popular logo artists charge $45 an hour or more. Most projects take days to weeks to complete. However, some clients have a set budget and timeframe in mind, so you might make between $100 to $200 per project. The enigma of freelance work is that the jobs vary, so there are no set of rules on how much you can make. Also, Upwork requires you to show work progress as you go along, so make sure you are keeping up with the tasks or milestones. If you like creating logos and art and want to focus on that path, once you get experience and good reputation, you could make six-figures by just creating logos.

Build a strong portfolio. Potential clients will check your profile and your rate while scanning for new freelancers. If you create original and interesting logos for your profile, a client will most likely be willing to pay your rate.

NFT's are another way to make income with Midjourney. We are only going to touch upon this subject since it can be more complex than the other methods. It involves creating unique pieces of creative work and "selling" them on a trade market. An NFT (non-fungible token) is a unique digital asset that is stored on a blockchain. You will need to create a volume of art pieces (more than 50, some have 200+) and then post them on an NFT marketplace site such as opensea.com. After you post your content, buyers who like your art can purchase it using a cryptocurrency called Ethereum. Ethereum is a decentralized open source blockchain system that features its own cryptocurrency similar to Bitcoin. The steps to making money on OpenSea are:

- Create an OpenSea account and connect your Ethereum wallet.

- Create or mint an NFT.

- Set a price for your NFT.

- List your NFT for sale.

- Wait for someone to buy your NFT.

- Receive the sale price in your Ethereum wallet.

If you are very creative, you can create different pieces of art that are unique and in demand. If you become one of the more popular artists, you can make over ten thousand a month selling your art. There have been a few outlier occasions where artists made millions of dollars by selling their art. We shouldn't exactly count on this, but if someone else did it, then it's possible it can happen for you.

Once you sell your art, you will get Ethereum deposited in your wallet, which you can then send to a cryptocurrency exchange platform such as Binance to convert to USD. There are also transaction and "gas" fees involved with cryptocurrency. There is a steeper learning curve to selling NFT's, but if you are interested in it, then you should check out YouTube and watch beginner explainer videos or check out *The NFT Handbook* by Jason Teutsch and Ashley Teutsch. It should help you get a good understanding of the space.

Also, you can get Midjourney prompt samples by using a tool called Describe. This will give you prompts based on the image you upload. Here are the steps:

Step 1: Type /describe in the prompt box

Step 2: Upload the image

Step 3: Prompt results will process

Step 4: Generate variations of the images

Describe is a good way to get prompt ideas if you have images you like, but don't know how to describe them in the prompt field.

We've explored a few of the more sustainable ways to make money using Midjourney. There are more, but these are some of the more profitable and reliable methods. Midjourney is an excellent platform to create vivid and original images with just a few descriptive words. It is an amazing step in AI technology that we can use to build more income. If you are creative, become skilled, and use one of the chatbots to effectively create attractive marketing pieces, it is completely possible to make over $100,000 a year using Midjourney and a couple other AI tools.

Leonardo.AI

Leonardo.ai is another AI art creation tool that can be used to generate a variety of creative content, including images, illustrations, and even 3D models. Leonardo.ai does similar tasks to Midjourney, but Leonardo has a different look in its creations, and the user-interface is easier to manage.

In my opinion, Leonardo is more suited for cartoon art, illustrations, and animation characters. It's also similar to Midjourney in that we will use text-to-image prompts to create digital art. In Leonardo, the prompts can be simpler, since there are no parameter prompts such as changing aspect ratio or style. This can be done by selecting the corresponding button on the left-hand menu. Let's take a look at the interface.

Firstly, head over to leornardo.ai and create an account and select a username. It asks for your interests, but these don't really have a bearing on your creations. Once you create an account, you'll be in the main dashboard. Like Midjourney, your creations will be public unless you pay for an account that lets you generate private images.

To start creating images, click the Image Generation link.

Welcome to Leonardo.Ai
Get started
Let's pick your @username
@ myawesomeusername
Username must be between 4-15 characters and contain letters, numbers and underscores only.
What are your interests?
Must select at least one.
Advertising
Architecture
Art
Board Games
Education
Fashion
Film Tv
Interior Design
Marketing
Product Design
Stock Images
Video Games
Other
I confirm that I am over 18 and want to show NSFW content by default
Next

Leonardo.Ai
150
Upgrade
Start Here
Home
Community Feed
Personal Feed
Training & Datasets
Finetuned Models
User Tools
AI Image Generation
AI Canvas BETA
Texture Generation ALPHA
Featured Models
DreamShaper v7
Lykon is back with another update. This model is great at a range of different styles.
Leonardo
3D Animation Style
Great at 3D film vibes, capable of complex scenes with rich color. Storyboard time!
Leonardo
Recent Creations
Search gallery
Search
All
Upscaled

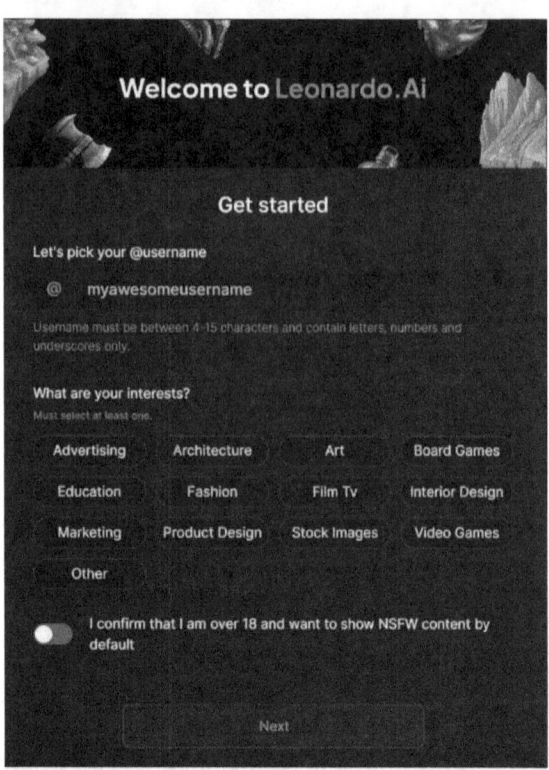

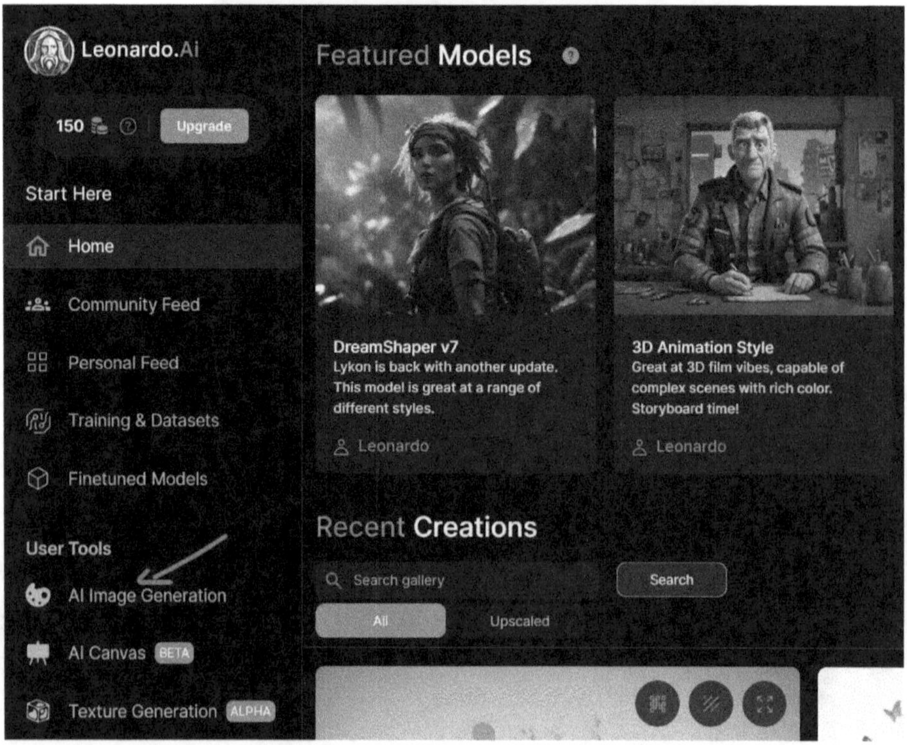

Here you will be able to create images based on your text prompts. On the left-hand side, you can use several settings to help customize your images.

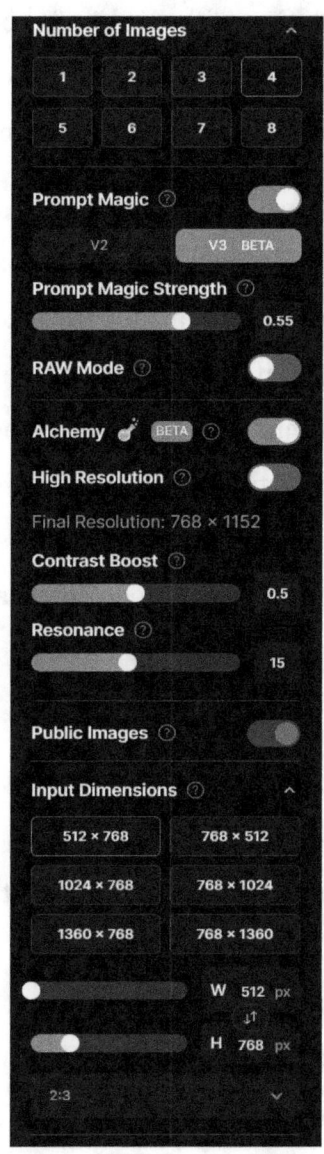

Number of Images is the number of generated images the platform will generate. Unlike Midjourney that is set at four, here you can select 1-8 images per generation. Remember that more image generation means more credits used. One of the perks of Leonardo.ai is that you get 150 credits that regenerate every day, so you can use all your credits to make images, then come back the next day to make more for free.

Prompt Magic is unique to Leonardo and helps to increase the likelihood of the platform generating the image based on the prompt details. It gives more detail to the image and "listens" to your prompt more closely. For example, if your prompt is "red car with tinted windows, detailed," you might get images that have the red car with a driver or the red car on the street. If you use Prompt Magic, most likely there will just be the car and that's it, as it adheres to the prompt more strictly and doesn't try to fill in with added details. Prompt Magic Strength is how strong the prompt magic will be. It's best just to leave it on the default setting unless your images aren't as detailed as you want.

The next important setting is Alchemy. This is a setting exclusive to Leonardo and gives images more details, contrast, vibrance and resolution. It can dramatically change the look of the images. You should try out the prompts with Alchemy off first to learn which prompts are looking good for your project, then turn it on since it uses more credits and there is a limit to how many images you can generate with the free plan.

The next settings can be left at default for now. The more important settings are Public Images and Input Dimensions. When you have the free plan, your images are public. Other users will be able to see them and the prompts you use. This is fine for now and you can learn from other users. However, if you are going to use a lot of images for business and to earn revenue, then you should upgrade to make them exclusive.

Next is Input Dimensions. This will be the aspect ratio of the images. Generally, you want higher dimension images. This is because you might want to use the image for different means in the future and scaling could be an issue. If you have a high aspect ratio image, you can scale down without losing many details. On the other hand, scaling up from low dimension image can lead to pixelation and loss of quality. There are free AI image upscaling websites that can upscale the images without losing quality such as **upscale.media**. However, personally I like to generate images in higher dimension sizes to be sure the quality output is as high as possible. You can also convert an image to an SVG (scalable vector graphic) which you can scale up or down without quality loss since there are no pixels. However, sometimes there is a loss of quality when converting.

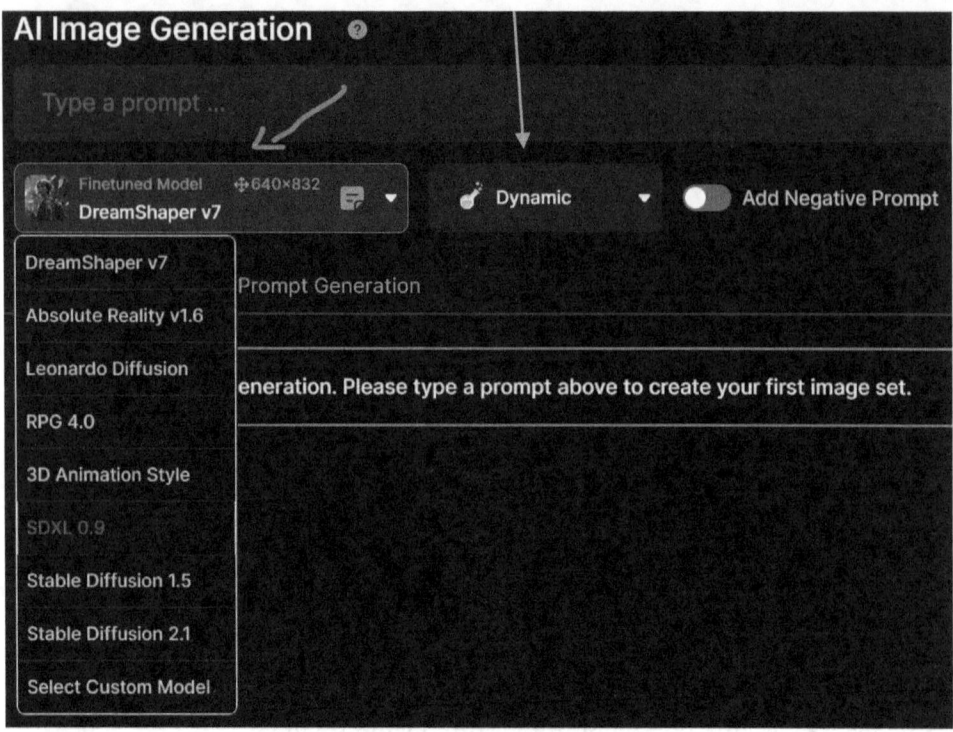

Finetuned Model will change the look of the images greatly, and should be experimented with to find the best choice for your project. There are a few different options, and for most uses, the top three options will often be used.

Each of these models has their own creative look, and each has a subset of independent creative choices. There are selections such as Dynamic, Anime, Creative, and Photograph. Each of these has its own look and should be customized based on the project. If there isn't a specific look you need, just leave it on the default or None. You can see samples at the top, under Featured Models.

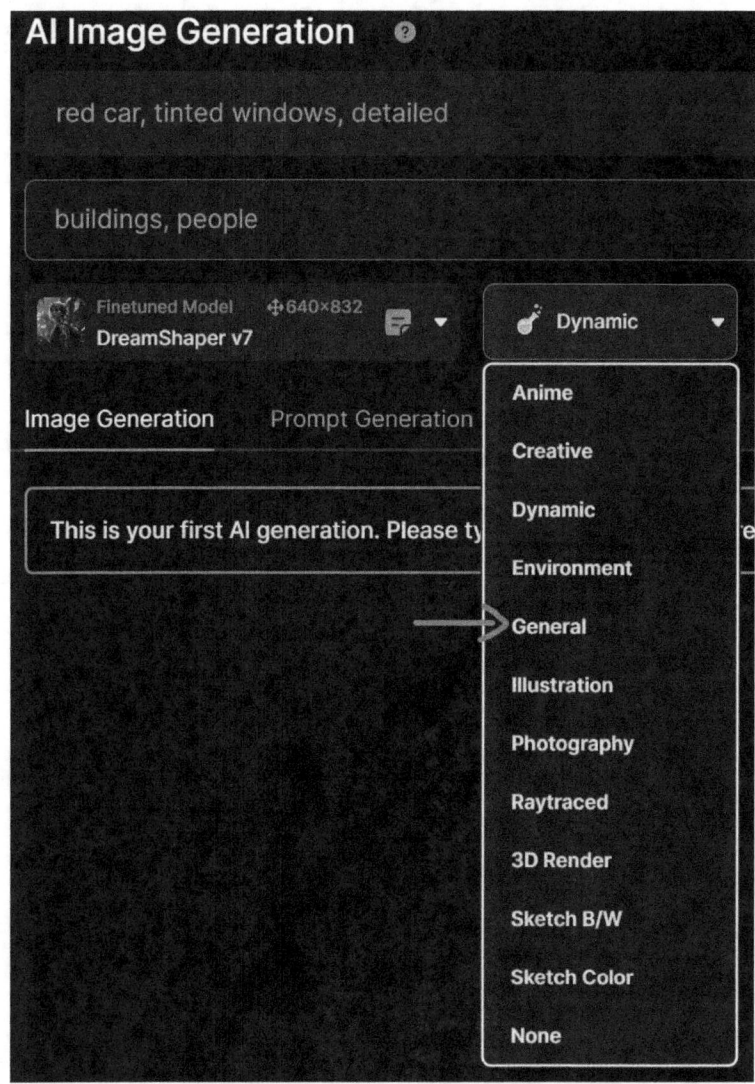

To start out, we can use DreamShaper model and General for the subset. DreamShaper has a good mix of photorealism and animation. Also, this will produce a standard image and is a good way to test out prompts until you find some that you'll use regularly.

For the first prompt, I typed in "red car, tinted windows, detailed."

In the Negative Prompt, I typed in "people, buildings" because I don't want those aspects in the image.

Here is the result:

We got a pretty nice car with reflections and details. However, it looks a little dark and I want more of the car body. To achieve this, hover over the bottom of the image and click Unzoom. You can also select Edit to edit the image in Canvas and change details, as well as remove the background. They all cost tokens, so make sure you want to use the image before spending tokens.

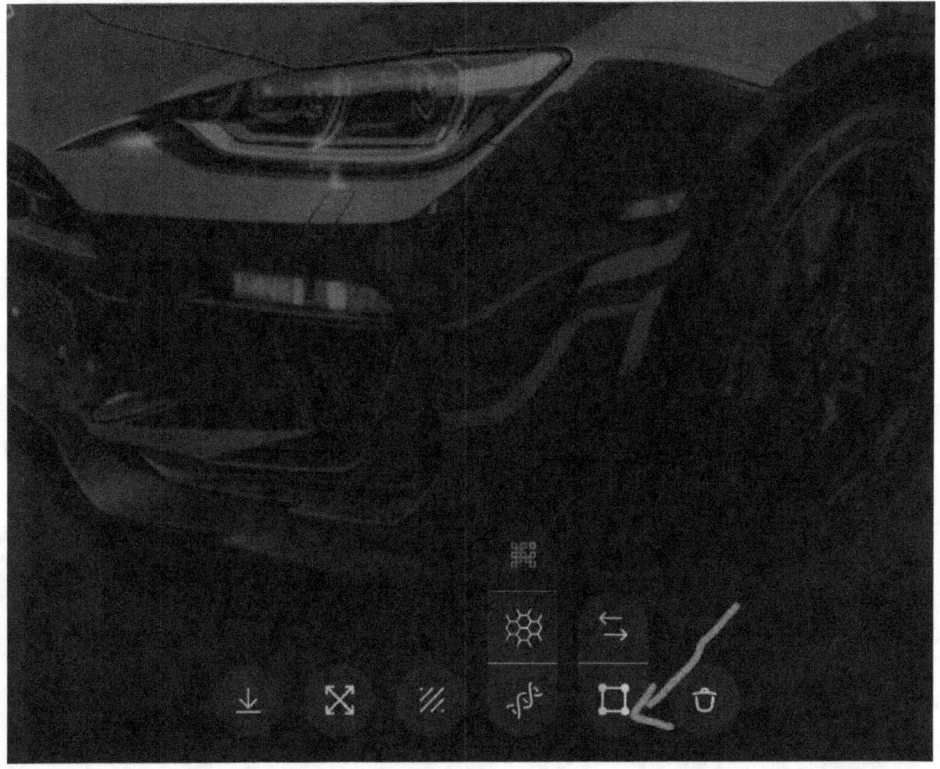

If the Unzoom doesn't fix the problem, go into Canvas and select the movable box in the center. Move the box to the end of the image, but make sure some of the image is covered. This will help the platform take data from the original image and expand the details. In the prompt box, I put in the same prompt text as the original: red car, tinted windows, detailed.

After generating, we can see the platform has expanded the details and made more of the car body visible. Be sure to keep a little of the image within the box.

Based off the original, I was able to expand the image and add more details to the image, and also created more of the body of the car. Here is a comparison:

The original.

The image I edited in canvas is next.

We have almost a full car now and didn't change a word in the prompt box. The edit in canvas option is a good tool to use if you need to finetune an image and don't want to create a new one or if you need to expand on an existing image.

If you find that you're not getting the results you want from a prompt, there is an option. Go to the prompt box and click Prompt Generation. In this box, I typed in **red car with tinted windows**, and selected the number of responses to generate. The platform generated four prompts to use:

	red car with tinted windows
1	A sleek, cherry-red sports car with darkly tinted windows, parked in a dimly lit alleyway.
2	A vintage, fire-engine red convertible with smoky-black windows, glinting in the bright sunlight.
3	A glossy, candy-apple red sedan with deep-blue tinted windows, parked in a bustling city street.
4	A rusty, faded-red hatchback with lightly-tinted windows, parked in a quiet suburban neighborhood.

If you like one of the prompts, you can select Generate which is to the right or you can take some of the text and add or improve the prompt. Prompt Generation is a good feature to use if you are having trouble coming up with prompts, and are not producing the results you want. Prompt Generations don't use tokens and you can use up to 1,000, so you shouldn't worry about running out.

Now that you have a basic understanding of Leonardo, now it's time to talk about how we can use this tool to make us another revenue source. Much like Midjourney, Leonardo lets you use any image you create for commercial purposes, so that's exactly what we're going to do. One way we can make money is to use our prompt skills to create book cover designs. Use freelance sites such as Fiverr, Upwork and 99 Designs. You can create a profile and apply as a designer. Make a few samples, then have Jasper or ChatGPT write a profile bio for you. Once accepted, you can start searching for clients.

*Note that all freelance sites take a percentage of the final payout as an expense for using their platform and finding clients. 99 Designs charges more than the others, so it's best to use all three to maximize revenue potential.

Once you set-up your accounts, learned how to use the image creation, and ready to help clients, then it's time to start marketing. You can create a Facebook and Instagram profile and upload sample images of your book cover art. Video doesn't work so well in this genre, so stick to image heavy sources, especially Instagram. Create a portfolio of work that are in popular genres, and add at least 5 images to start. Then add 2-3 per week subsequently.

Also, check out Amazon and Barnes & Noble to learn different book cover styles. Look at the most popular books and take note of common charateristics and features of the covers. There are a few add-ons that lets you reverse prompt images, so all you will need to do is upload an image and the app will build prompts based on the image. Prompt Perfect is one tool for Leonardo. Remember, you don't want to copy, just imitate and replicate with your own personal creativity.

Another avenue you can use to generate revenue is to sell AI art online. The most common site to sell digital art is Etsy. **You can also sell on redbubble.com, pixelsmerch.com, and society6.com** but let's talk about Etsy since they have millions of customers that shop on the site every month.

You can sell different types of art such as digital art, 3D art, and print art. Digital art is easier since you just need to create the artwork and upload it. There is nothing more to do. Print art requires either printing yourself and shipping (difficult) or use a print-on-demand service such as printful.com or theprintspace.com. You can use these services to dropship your art. When someone buys your art on Etsy, you can send it to one of the sites to print and ship. You can charge more for services such as framing, larger prints, and mounting options.

When selling digital art, it takes some time and effort. You will need to do basic search exploration to see what is popular to sell. You can do this by going to Etsy, and in the search bar type "digital prints." You can see there are millions of results.

6,933,238 results, with Ads ⑦   Sort by: Relevancy ▾

It would be nearly impossible to rank on the first couple of pages as a new seller. That's why we need to niche down to reduce the number of competition. One way to do this is to narrow down your search and carve out niches that have only a few thousand results. One way I did this was to use **landmarks**. I typed in "Mount Rushmore digital art." Only a couple hundred results showed up.

190 results, with Ads ⑦ ⟨ Sort by: Top Customer Reviews ▾ ⟩

I then typed in "Florida beach digital art." A few thousand results populated and some sellers have thousands of reviews.

7,014 results, with Ads ⑦ ⟨ Sort by: Relevancy ▾ ⟩

Don't just stick to the U.S. go international. I typed in Eiffel Tower and there were 1,206 results, including those with ads. That's not bad competition. Make straight art and also create unique art with orginal designs. Customers are likely to be interested in art that they can't get elsewhere.

Once you found a few ideas for your work, then it's time to create captivating listings. Head over to ChatGPT or even better, Jasper AI. I say this because Jasper has specfic templates that utilizes algorithms to help products rank higher in search pages for ecommerce. Once you are in the Jasper, go to the Dashboard then in Templates click Product Descriptions:

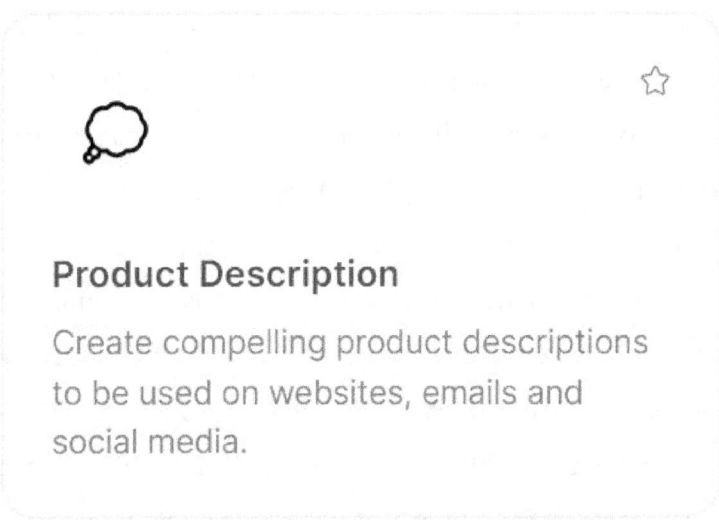

Product Description

Create compelling product descriptions to be used on websites, emails and social media.

I typed **"full product description for a digital art listing of the Eiffel Tower. Use high-ranking keywords and optimize it for search."** Japer wrote a nice product description, here is a sample:

"This digital art piece is crafted with meticulous attention to detail, capturing the intricate architecture of the Eiffel Tower. The sweeping lines and bold silhouette of the tower stand out against a backdrop that features the soft hues of a Parisian sunset, creating a striking contrast that is sure to catch the eye."

That's a pretty nice description, and it only took ten seconds. Once you have your product descriptions, then it's time to add images. Images are the most important aspect in creating effective product listings. You will need to have at least six images to have an efficient listing, but the more the better. Try to make as many as the listing allows. Since you are selling digital art, it's best to put some type of watermark on the image before uploading so it doesn't get copied. Also, most digital art listings have a mockup of what the image would look like printed and framed. Many buyers will buy the digital file, then print and frame themselves. So, it's good to give them an idea of what it will look like. You can get many mockup files from sites such as placeit.com or if you bought the subscription, from Envato Elements. Envato has hundreds of mockups that you can use for almost every product such as t-shirts, clothing, mugs, stickers, hats, bags, and pretty much any merchandise that you intend to sell. See the previous image?

I found this professional looking picture mockup on Envato Elements. I then created a picture of the Eiffel Tower in both Jasper AI and Leonardo AI to compare. Remember that you can create AI images in Jasper AI as well.

This photo was created with Jasper. It has beautiful details and the lighting is exquisite.

I then loaded up Adobe Photoshop and dragged in the mockup file, then the Eiffel Tower photo. After that, I clicked the Quick Selection tool and with a couple of clicks, I had an outline inside the mockup picture frame. Then once the quick selection is made, I pressed delete to remove the inside of the frame.

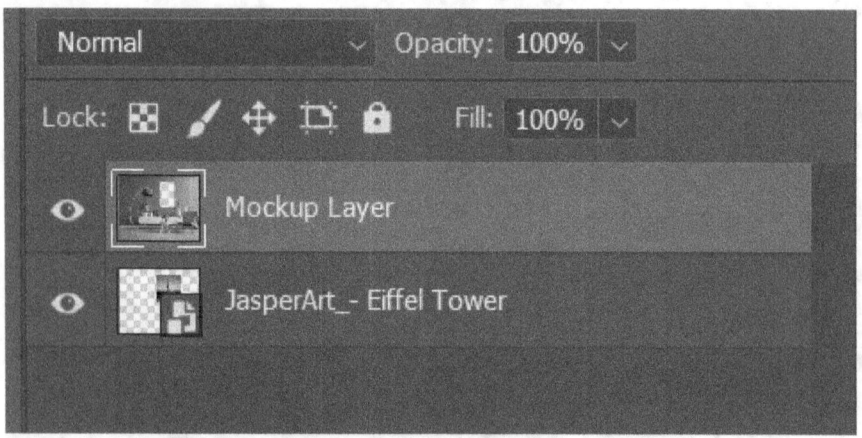

After that, I simply dragged the Eiffel Tower photo to the frame. Fit it inside and then drag the image layer underneath the mockup layer to get a picture-perfect mockup.

I then did the same thing for the Leonardo image:

You decide which is better!

If the image doesn't fit, simply drag it by the corner points to resize it until it fits. You won't lose any of the details. So just like that we have gorgeous digital art mockups! Very lifelike and vivid. This can be a great addition to your product listings since they give the customer a compelling representation of what their product will look like.

After you make enough images and have captivating product descriptions, then it's time to publish your art. Etsy has the distinction of favoring sellers who have lots of listings. It's recommended to have at least 10, and a good range is between 10-20 listings. It costs $.20 cents to list each item, so if you choose to list twenty items it will cost about $4. Etsy also takes a cut of the sales, but since you're selling digital products, you don't have to worry about shipping or insurance. You can also add a no return policy if needed, but most people like to have this option available. Digital art doesn't sell for big prices, so it's good to focus on volume. Let's check out an example.

 If you list 20 prints and have 8 high performers that sell 5 copies a week, that's 40 sales per week. If your net revenue is $5 for each sale, then that's about $800 a month from selling digital art. That's a nice amount for just creating free pictures. This example is on the low-end, but it does show how you can make nice extra income for a limited amount of work. Also, we used Etsy as example, the other sites I mentioned can bring more sales too. Let's say you sell art on 4 different sites and make $500 a month on each. That's $2,000 a month for just selling digital art.

In addition to selling digital art, you can create designs and market them as print-on-demand products. One of the more popular types of print on demand is t-shirts. Custom t-shirts have been around for a while and some have made seven-figure businesses just from shirts. One of the reasons for this is the design of the shirt. Years ago it was more difficult to create designs and you had to have some form of illustrative talent. Today, we can use AI and our imagination to make creative art for custom products.

One of the more popular print on demand companies is Printful.com. I like them because they make quality products and have fast processing and shipping. You will need to connect a store for dropshipping, since they don't offer a direct commerce option. One of the good things about Printful is that it can connect to all major e-commerce platforms such as WIX, WordPress, and Etsy. Since we already created an Etsy account and it's pretty much free to use, lets use them.

You will go through the same process as we did for the artwork. This time we are going to search for t-shirts that sell well but have low competition. I searched at the top of the page through "Womens" then "Tops" then "T-Shirts." As of today, there are over 7 million results. I then typed in the search bar "ski tshirt." There were just over 12,000 results with ads.

12,303 results, with Ads ⑦ (Sort by: Relevancy ▾)

Since we're going to use unique designs, we should be able to stand out. A good rule of thumb is to sell products that have between 4,000 to 12,000 results. The lower the better, but too low and there might not be a demand. Running ads is relatively cheap and can help boost sales. It's possible to get higher ranking based on descriptive long-tail keywords and ads.

For this idea, I headed back to Midjourney and used the prompt "fun skiing, graphic t shirt--s 750." I got a nice image that I think would look great on a t-shirt and other products.

Now that I have a design, it's time to see how it looks on a shirt. One of the perks of using Printful is that they offer their own mockups to use, but if you want to use your own you can. I made a quick mockup in Photoshop since I already have the templates. Here is the result:

The shirt has nice color and vivid illustration. If you're a ski fan, then you will probably like the design and appearance. If we use an image like this for a main product image, it should catch the eye and will most likely stop a shopper from scrolling and take a look at the listing. If you have a collection of top quality images, an optimized listing, and competitive pricing, you should start to get views which turns into sales. Running ads at first is a good idea, then turn them off once you start making sales since you'll start to organically rank higher in the search. Companies such as Etsy, Amazon, Walmart, etc. mostly put the high selling products on the first pages. This is because they receive a percentage every time a product is sold, so it makes more sense for them to put high performing products on top so they can get their commission. Etsy and Printful will take their cuts too, so it's important to calculate your selling price to make sure your profit margins are high. Printful has a nice calculator to use to help with this. If priced right, the average net profit for a print on demand shirt should be $6 - $10 per shirt. There is no cost to set-up a Printful account and they only take a fee after you start receiving orders.

Now you have another product and a listing idea.

Remember how Etsy likes lots of products? You can create different product listings like t-shirts and artwork, which all counts towards your store's SEO performance. If you want to create different stores on Etsy, you can. For example, if you want to start an art only store to bring in art lover customers, you can. If you name your store Jimmy's Book Shop, then it wouldn't make much sense to sell clothing or stickers. You will just need to sign-up for a new account with a new email. As of writing, Etsy allows this practice, so you can have multiple niche stores earning you multiple streams of income. According to Etsy's statistics, top earners can make multiple six-figures a year with their products.

As we've seen in the previous examples, AI image generation is a fascinating and powerful tool we can utilize to enhance our chances of earning more income. The important part is to leverage the tools properly to maximize earning potential.

VIDEO AI

We have talked about writing great copy and creating outstanding images. Now we are going to make exceptional videos. According to some marketing studies, videos are recognized more than 95% more than picture or text and they are much more effective in converting into a sale. This means that having fascinating and effective video is much more likely to have a lasting effect on your clients compared to other means. Let's be honest, if we had to either read a 5-paragraph product description or watch a 2-minute product video, most people would choose the video. We are just wired that way. Video engages more of our senses and allows us to absorb the information more thoroughly.

Currently there are a few easy-to-use video AI programs out there, and it seems like new ones are popping up every week. Although there are good programs out there, I don't use or would recommend any that don't offer a free trial to test it out. If you have ever made marketing videos with stock video, you know it takes a long time to find and edit the videos. With AI video makers, the videos are created automatically in a matter of minutes. That's why one of the recommended programs for making captivating videos is Pictory.

Pictory

Pictory lets you create videos with just an email address, they just limit the length of the video and how many projects you can create.

However, the pricing is very manageable. We can use Pictory to create videos with stock video that can explain whatever product you want to use. Much like Midjourney that creates images from text, Pictory uses text to make video.

According to their official description, Pictory lets you:

- Input your script that generates into video

- Add visuals from our large library of stock images

- Add AI voice-overs

- Add your own voice-over, and auto-sync it with your project at the click of a button

- Apply styles and branding

- Change aspect ratio of your videos

- Create your own templates, for future use

These are great features that we will need to make great looking AI videos.

Let's try using ChatGPT with Pictory.

I am using this prompt for ChatGPT: "Can you write a one paragraph product ad, descriptive and conversational for electric bikes?" I pasted the response in the script editor.

One of the main features of Pictory is that you can highlight certain words in the script for emphasis and the program will find relevant videos based on the descriptive words in your script. You don't need to find stock video and assemble yourself, Pictory does everything automatically.

After you paste the script in the editor, you will go to the video template section. Here you will choose which template you like the best.

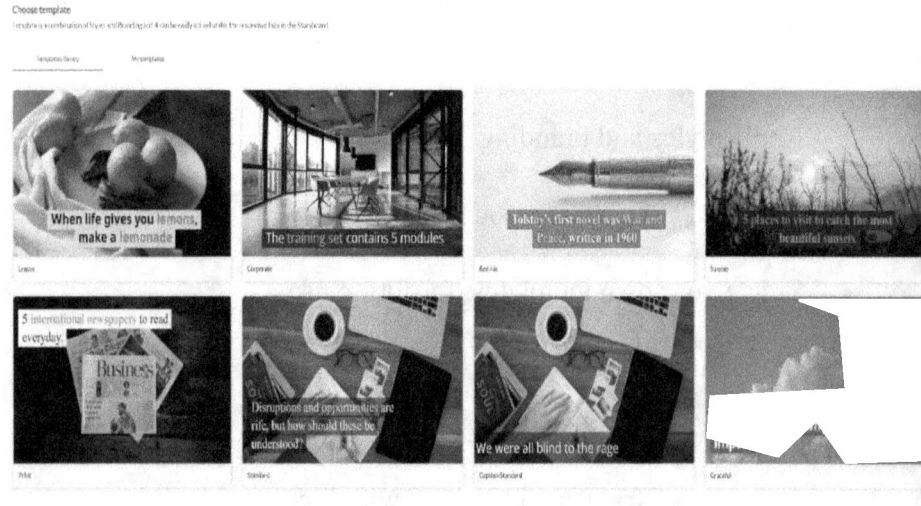

I chose the metro template and 16:9 aspect ratio because I'm going to use it for YouTube.

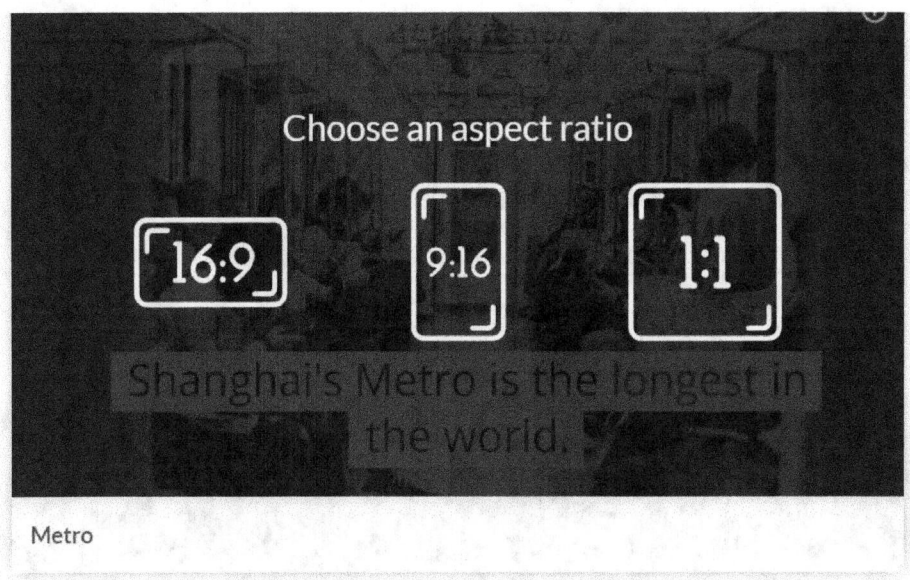

Metro

The platform will create video with captions based on the text, but it's not going to be completely accurate. We will need to add a few clips by searching the text bar at the top.

I typed in "electric bike" and got several responses. I liked the first choice, so I clicked on it to add to the intro. You will see the different scenes in the right panel.

The video I chose is a nice overhead view of a man riding an electric bike. It's a nice action shot that can grab the viewers' attention, so that's why I put it at the beginning. Remember, you should always start off videos as either exciting or informatively enticing, so it gives the viewer a reason to keep watching.

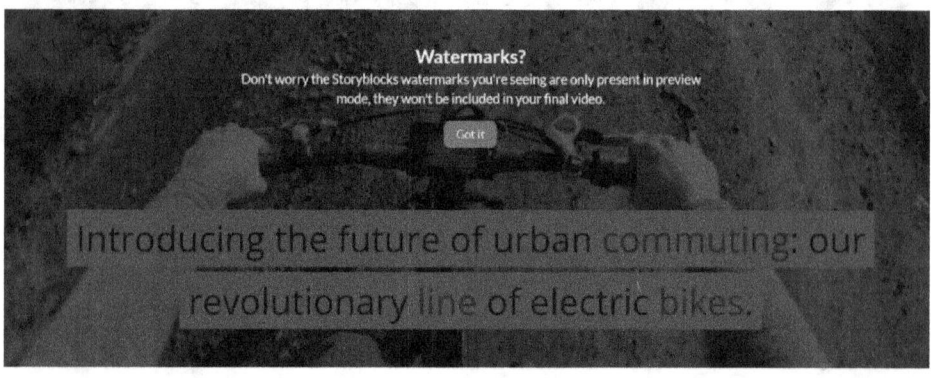

My current video has seven scenes excluding the intro and outro. I just went through the scenes and kept the videos that I liked. The ones I didn't like, I just clicked on the scene then clicked the video that I found in the search to replace them. There were over a hundred electric bike results and I only needed 3. We can make a lot of captivating videos using this method without the fear of repeating the same footage over and over.

Once I had my videos ready, I went to the left panel to select other options. There are several options to choose from including: adding elements, audio, text, style, branding and aspect ratio. Elements is where we can add emoticons, GIFs, and stickers. I'm not going to add any emoticons or stickers since I think the video and text are enough, so now I'm going to go to the audio section. The audio panel is where we can change the background music, add voice-over, and add custom audio. If you want to record the voice-over yourself instead of using an AI voice, you can add it here. First, I'm going to change the background music. I'm going to change it to something that is more energetic and action oriented.

I changed the mood to "intense" and found some great tracks.

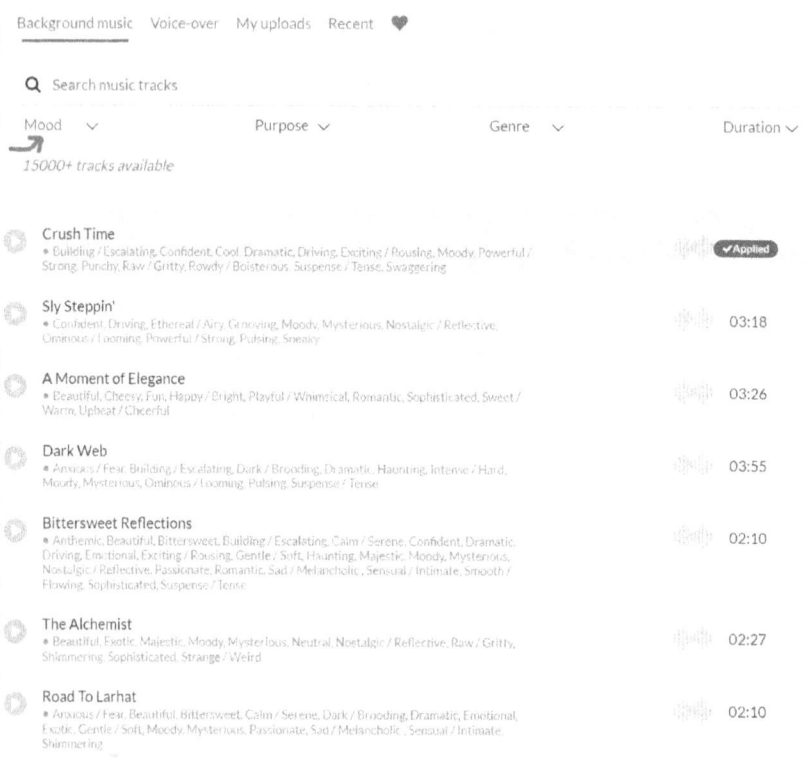

Background music   Voice-over   My uploads   Recent   ♥

Q   Search music tracks

Mood   ⌄   Purpose ⌄   Genre   ⌄   Duration ⌄

15000+ tracks available

Crush Time
• Building / Escalating, Confident, Cool, Dramatic, Driving, Exciting / Rousing, Moody, Powerful / Strong, Punchy, Raw / Gritty, Rowdy / Boisterous, Suspense / Tense, Swaggering   ✔ Applied

Sly Steppin'
• Confident, Driving, Ethereal / Airy, Grooving, Moody, Mysterious, Nostalgic / Reflective, Ominous / Looming, Powerful / Strong, Pulsing, Sneaky   03:18

A Moment of Elegance
• Beautiful, Cheesy, Fun, Happy / Bright, Playful / Whimsical, Romantic, Sophisticated, Sweet / Warm, Upbeat / Cheerful   03:26

Dark Web
• Anxious / Fear, Building / Escalating, Dark / Brooding, Dramatic, Haunting, Intense / Hard, Moody, Mysterious, Ominous / Looming, Pulsing, Suspense / Tense   03:55

Bittersweet Reflections
• Anthemic, Beautiful, Bittersweet, Building / Escalating, Calm / Serene, Confident, Dramatic, Driving, Emotional, Exciting / Rousing, Gentle / Soft, Haunting, Majestic, Moody, Mysterious, Nostalgic / Reflective, Passionate, Romantic, Sad / Melancholic, Sensual / Intimate, Smooth / Flowing, Sophisticated, Suspense / Tense   02:10

The Alchemist
• Beautiful, Exotic, Majestic, Moody, Mysterious, Neutral, Nostalgic / Reflective, Raw / Gritty, Shimmering, Sophisticated, Strange / Weird   02:27

Road To Larhat
• Anxious / Fear, Beautiful, Bittersweet, Calm / Serene, Dark / Brooding, Dramatic, Emotional, Exotic, Gentle / Soft, Moody, Mysterious, Passionate, Sad / Melancholic, Sensual / Intimate, Shimmering   02:10

I found one that I really liked, so I selected it. Now it's time for the actual voice of the video. When working on YouTube videos, audio is just as important as the video quality. No matter how interesting or pleasing a video may look, if the audio is not clear, I simply can't watch it.

In the voice-overs section, there are a few dozen voices to choose from. They have male/female, English, English UK, Australian,

New Zealand, Indian and South African dialects. I like the Arthur (UK) voice so I clicked apply, and now that voice will speak the words of our ChatGPT created script and combine it with stock electric bike footage.

I then went into the text option and added a simple text to the 1st video.

Then I went into "styles." This is where you can change the style of the text and color of the captions. You can see, the program chose to emphasize certain words in the text.

I like the yellow background color, but I'm going to change the intro style. I added a nice red background fill color to the text and also changed the style. To do this, simply click on the Intro scene in the scene builder window, then click the Styles Library.

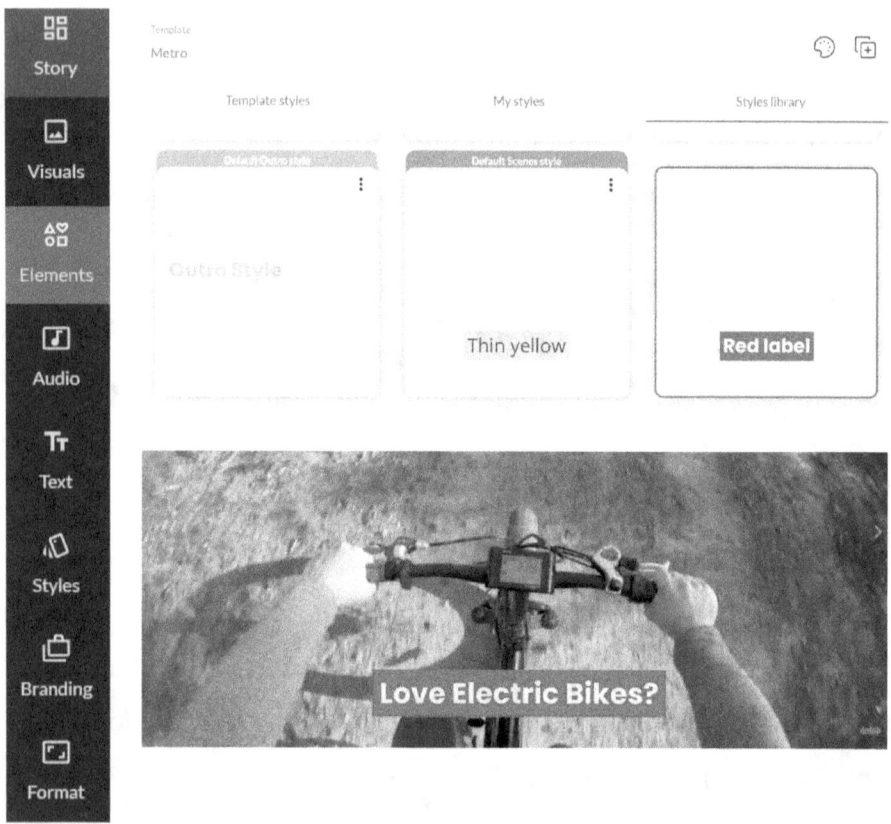

I found this style near the middle. So far, it's looking pretty good.

Lastly, there is the Branding panel. Here you can add your own custom branding materials such as a logo, custom video or picture for your intro or outro, and custom text. This is good to use if you have a custom logo opener video or have a brand text you want to use in your videos.

Now that everything is ready, just click preview to view the sample. You can preview each scene independently or the entire project.

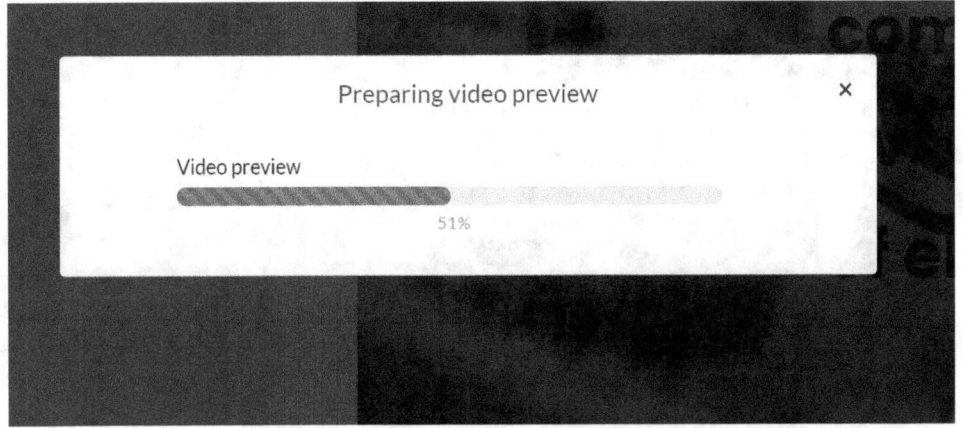

Here is an image of the final result:

It looks great and sounds amazing. The AI voice is seamless and rich. Some AI voices have a tendency to sound stilted and artificial. With Pictory, it sounds natural. Also, don't worry about the watermarks, those go away with a paid subscription.

So I just created a realistic and captivating 90-second video using descriptive text, audio, and video in less than five minutes. I can use this video for a blog post, YouTube, or as a video ad. When using video, it's a good idea to take longer videos and cut them up into smaller versions and post them on various social media sites.

This is known as repurposing and can increase your overall social presence. If you make a five-minute video, you can post that video on YouTube, edit out a minute or two and post on TikTok, take the same minute and post as a YouTube Short and an Instagram Reel or Story. You can also post as a Facebook video to capture all major social media opportunities. From one video, you can get 4-5 relevant uses. Repurpose all your long-form videos to get the most out of them. There are some sites that repurpose your videos, but they usually charge a fee. Unless you're making a good amount of money and don't have the time, it's best to edit yourself and then post. What's important about this technique is that the more your content is posted and engaged with, the higher your future content will rank in search engines.

Let's say you want to dropship electric bikes, so you start a YouTube channel all about electric bikes. You spend about an hour making around ten five-minute electric bike videos with Pictory. If you post about two - three videos a week on YouTube. That is about a month of content. From those videos, you can edit out three, one-minute sections of the more interesting parts from one video. So now you have three 1-minute clips from one 5-minute long video. If you post your long videos on Monday and Friday, you can post YouTube Shorts Tuesday, Wednesday, and Thursday, for example.

You can post the full videos on Facebook Monday and Friday, then take the edited clips and upload them as Feed Videos on the opposite days or upload the full-length videos as IGTV videos. So, from one video, you have at least five days' worth of content for every major social media platform, and it took less than ten minutes to complete. With all ten videos you have about a month's worth of material. If you are really ambitious, you can plan out your social media strategy and create six months' worth of material. Based on YouTube and most other social media statistics, it takes about six months of regular posts to build a strong following. If you create compelling content, you will see the subscribers and views slowly ramp up, and then there will be a point when your channel could explode. This is because YouTube will rank your channel higher in search and also for suggested views. The good thing is once that growth phase starts, the channel will build much faster in the following months. One of the perks of using social media is that you can schedule posts ahead of time. As of writing, there isn't really a limit on the number of scheduled YouTube videos or how far in advance you can schedule videos. The same is true for Facebook, and since Facebook owns Instagram, you can schedule your Facebook and Instagram posts concurrently up to a year in advance.

Just imagine if you post high-quality and engaging content for six months, it's completely in the realm of possibility to have thousands of subscribers in six months. Some channels have grown to have hundreds of thousands of subscribers in the same amount of time. It really depends on how popular your videos are, the keywords you use, and the professionalism of your content.

This doesn't include your Instagram, TikTok and Facebook followers. If you have six months' worth of quality content, you will be an authority on the subject, which search engines like.

We will continue with the electric bike example. Let's say you decide to start promoting your electric bike dropship store. You have a few thousand loyal subscribers who are now brand aware of your channel, which means they are aware of, familiar with, and dedicated to you and your subject. Those thousands are obviously interested in electric bikes and your subject matter and have also built trust in you. Once you start promoting your bikes, you'll have a few thousand interested clients. Of course, not everyone will buy your products, but **let's say about 5% out of 3,000 subscribers purchase a bike monthly. You sell the bike for $900 and the cost of goods with expenses totals $550. This means your net profit is $350 per bike. Five percent of 3,000 is 150. $350 x 150 is $52,500.** That's a pretty amazing profit for just a weekend of work! Obviously, this is just an example, and you have to have some business acumen about finding good suppliers and minimizing your expenses, but it is possible with the right moves. This doesn't include ad revenue you can receive from your channel (which won't be too much but still something) and it doesn't include the sales you can get when running ads.

As long as your product is good, customers are happy, and you post high-quality content regularly, you can have a steady business all online.

We can see that Pictory is an excellent service to use to make quality videos. Pictory can be used for just about every product or service you may be interested in. The fact that it's mainly automated, makes creating videos faster and more creative. You can create faceless YouTube and Instagram content in minutes and make profit. Pictory is definitely one program I recommend checking out.

HeyGen

Another video maker is HeyGen. This program can take regular still images and turn them into videos complete with speech. Let's see how it works. I went to heygen.com and created an account. You can try it out for free. I went to the Dashboard to the left and selected Shakespeare as the avatar.

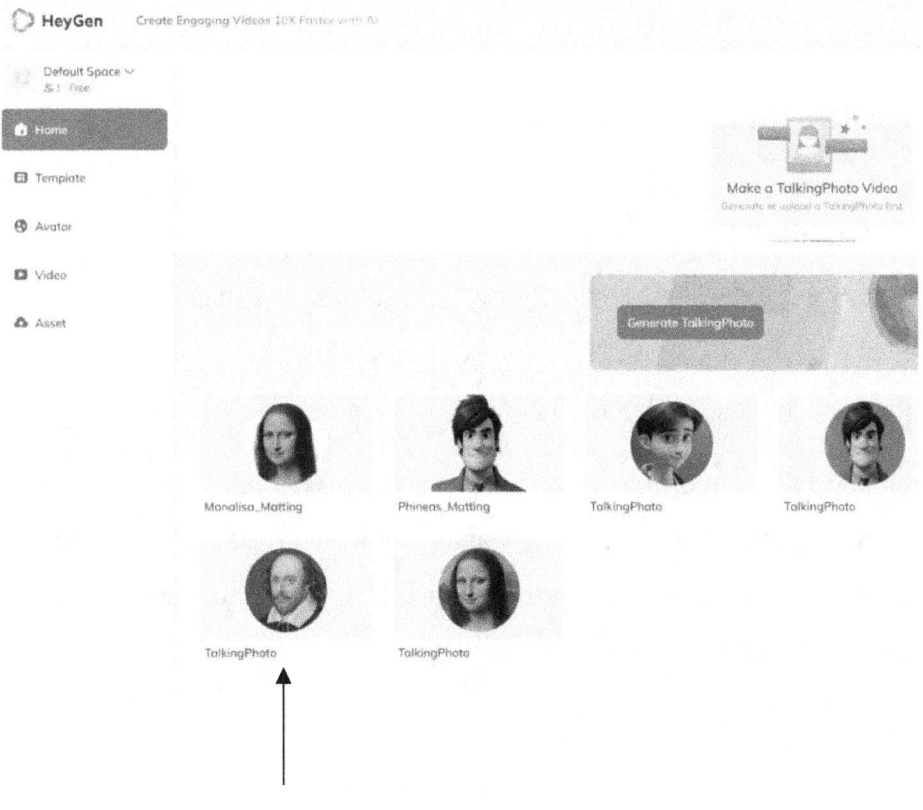

I selected the voice Keanan (UK) from the voice selection.

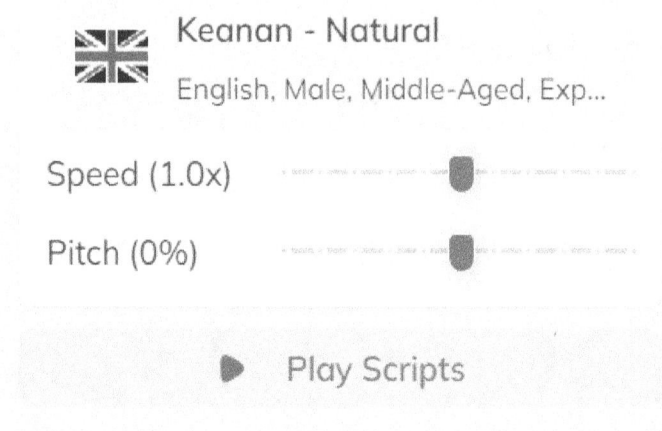

Just to test it out, I wrote the following text: "I am William Shakespeare, and I love electric bikes from Willy Shakes bike shop. It's the place to go for all your bike needs!"

Of course, I wouldn't use this in a real post, but it's fun to play around with the avatar. I clicked preview and it sounded great. The video won't play yet, so you just hear the voice. Once you are happy, just click the Submit button in the top right corner:

It takes a few minutes for the video to process, and once it's done you will get an email message stating it's ready. Depending on the length, it could take a few minutes. For this one-line video, the processing took about three minutes.

The video turned out pretty good, with full animation. The eyes were blinking, and mouth sync was accurate. There was even some head movement. So in just a few minutes we have a celebrity endorsement for our bike shop! ☺

HeyGen has over one hundred talking images and avatars. If you don't want to use an image, you can use one of the stock human avatars. These work the same way, and they can say whatever you program them to say. This is good for us to use as testimonials, how to videos, explainer videos, or even product reviews. The mouth and body movements are natural and realistic. You can select the voice you want or use your own. Everything is AI built and works the same as the previous Shakespeare example.

You can also add your own custom avatars. For example, for your videos you can create your own custom brand representative instead of paying for a spokesperson.

I went into Midjourney and asked the prompt to make a 3D render of a man's face for product videos. I got this render:

Not bad. He looks like an electric bike user. I can use this face for YouTube thumbnails or have him talk in the videos from the scripts we create in ChatGPT or Jasper.

I uploaded this image in HeyGen to create a custom avatar.

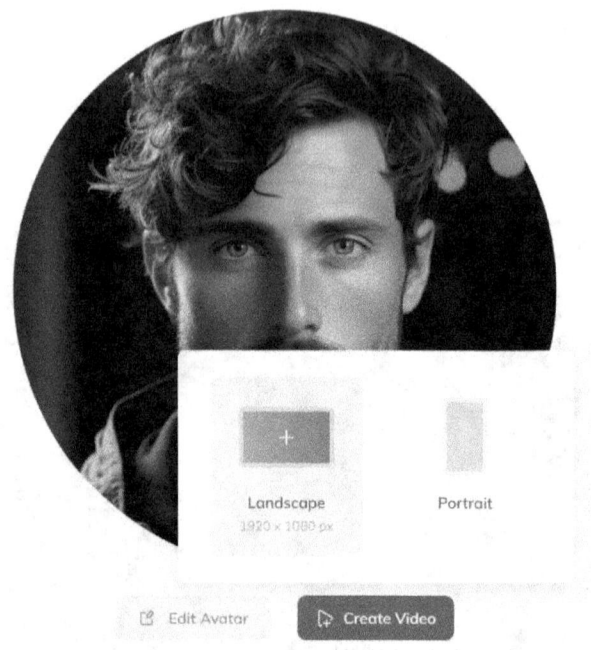

I changed the voice to Lucas (US), previewed and then submitted. After a few minutes I had a complete talking video from an image I created in Midjourney.

The image spoke the words I wrote for it and gave the proper intonation.

We can use this image as the face of our videos. By having a consistent character in our videos, it can give more recognition to our products and brand. Some people even use this tool to make Instagram posts of figures speaking inspirational quotes. In just a few months, they garnered tens of thousands of followers just by posting one minute videos. If you can create videos that are interesting and something people want to watch, it's possible to acquire thousands of subscribers in just a few months.

Another feature of HeyGen that I use often and has saved me a lot of time is the URL to Video feature. If you have an Amazon store, and want to convert your product descriptions to video, this feature will save you tons of time. All you have to do is copy & paste your Amazon link in the URL to Video section, and the platform will read your images, description, and bullet points and turn them into a video. You can post these videos on social media to increase brand awareness and authority. I took the paper towel link we used earlier and made this video:

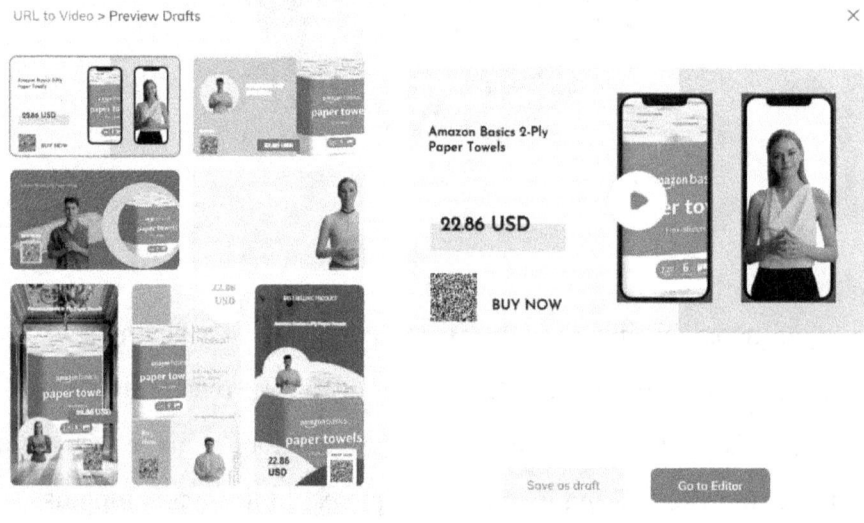

The video includes a talking avatar with custom voice, the price, images, and even a QR code to link to the product. You can edit everything in here as well, and is an excellent feature. Right now this feature is just for Amazon, but that will probably change in the future.

In addition to all these features, HeyGen also has a Text to Image feature similar to the AI image generators we reviewed. Type in what you want, and the platform will generate a realistic image. It isn't a dedicated tool, so it won't get too fancy, but you can create realistic appearing images and avatars.

There is also a ChatGPT plugin that works directly with HeyGen. You can type in what you need such as "create a short video about current real estate trends." The application will then create the script, audio, avatar, and complete video in a matter of minutes. Very simple. However, as of writing, you will need a paid ChatGPT account, so we won't delve into it, but I encourage you to research this plugin if you have ChatGPT Plus.

HeyGen has numerous templates to offer for your product or service. They have predesigned templates for e-commerce stores such as sports equipment, travel, and fitness. Incorporate an AI chatbot such as Jasper AI to write a compelling script, choose your custom avatar, and in a few minutes, you'll have an exciting video for your business. HeyGen offers free credits for new members, so you should be able to test out a few videos for free, but their pricing is one of the lowest for the quality and features you'll get. HeyGen is one AI video creator you should definitely check out.

DeepBrain AI Studios

Our next AI video creator is one of the more notable programs. DeepBrain is used by corporations such as Microsoft, Nvidia, and BMW. They even created an AI Howie Mandel character to interact with fans. DeepBrain is similar to Pictory and HeyGen, however there are a few exclusive advantages of using DeepBrain.

Much like Pictory, DeepBrain can create fully produced video complete with custom audio. However, DeepBrain includes the ability to use a custom talking avatar that is directly integrated with ChatGPT. So instead of going into ChatGPT and writing prompts, we just need to type in our subject in the DeepBrain prompt box and the program will add the subject script automatically. Let's try it out.

Head over to **deepbrain.io** then select Products then AI Studios. They have a few AI products, but for now, we're going to be using the video editor. Select Create a Video.

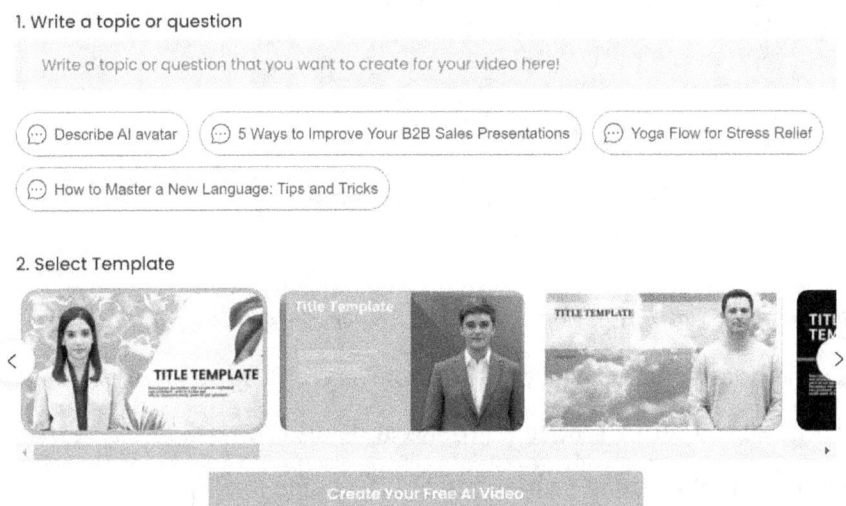

Here you can write your question, subject or prompt. There are several templates to choose from, but I'm going to create one from scratch. The prompt will coordinate with ChatGPT and the response will be added to the video. I typed in: "electric bike advertisement" and selected the male in the yellow shirt. Based on that prompt, DeepBrain made four slides with title and description.

One of the first things I changed was the background. I added a custom electric bike I created earlier in Midjourney, and added it to the background. I moved the text around and added a black rectangle to help highlight the text. I also changed the voice to Soft J Male. It sounded more appropriate for the subject. Since we can only test out one minute in the free plan, I took out a couple of slides, so now there are two.

This text was created automatically by ChatGPT in the prompt box. If you're not happy with it or want to edit it, you can simply do so by double-clicking the text, then type in the new text inside the field box. You can also change the color, size, etc. Like Pictory, you can add a background video, custom voice-over and use royalty free music. The downside is that DeepBrain doesn't have the most extensive royalty free audio library. In this case, you can use your Envato Elements account to download some tracks and grab some images if needed. You can use a motion video background if you want as well. I clicked on Export in the top right corner and after a couple of minutes, the video was produced. The platform produced a nice seamless video, complete with talking avatar, music and custom text.

With DeepBrain you can create video using the integrated ChatGPT function or use the "URL to video" function. You can simply paste the URL from a product page. The program will then take the text and information from the site and create a full-lenth video with speaking AI avatar. This is useful if you are selling products that have supplier pages, but don't have much details of the product. DeepBrain has more of a PowerPoint feel since it utilizes slides with text, but has the uniquness of utilizing AI avatars.

Overall, DeepBrain is a good platform that makes creating AI video fast and easy with a high customization factor. It's a nice combination of Pictory and HeyGen. They offer monthly and annual packages. Like most other AI video platforms, there is a discount on the annual subscription. You can always try the monthly option, and make as many videos as you can within your package limit and see if it will work for you. What I don't like about it is that the templates and avatars are a little limited right now, and if you want to create a lot of videos it will get expensive. This might change in the future though.

Use DeepBrain and other video AI platforms to create engaging videos for your stores, social media, and video ads. Fully customizable, talking avatars can be the next wave in marketing, so it's better to learn the format now, and get ahead of the competition.

AUDIO AI

We use AI to create videos, images and articles, so we need to discuss the fundamentals of using AI for audio and voice. Right now, there are a few audio platforms that can generate music and sound effects based on prompts similar to ChatGPT. However, most of these applications are not yet user-friendly and only generate 20 or so seconds, so we will not go too in-depth with them. Rather, we will explore the use of voice AI for our videos. Since audio needs to be as professional and high-quality as our videos, we need a platform that can make superb, realistic voices.

Murf AI

Like the other AI tools we explored, Murf AI can help you make money online through its advanced AI voice technology. Murf AI is a cloud-based text-to-speech platform that can generate over 120 voices in over 20 different languages. It can be used to create voice-over for social media posts such as YouTube, Instagram, Facebook, and TikTok. It can be used to make voices for webinars, online courses, tutorials, ads, explainer videos, courses and audiobooks. Since Murf AI is a dedicated voice generation platform, its focus on voice is evident in the quality of the audio. We can use voices from Murf AI and combine them with the videos we make on the video AI platforms. Let's check out the platform.

Firstly, head over to **murf.ai** and either create an account or log-in. I usually just sign-up using Google since it's faster. If you don't have a paid account, you can use the free plan to try out 10 minutes of audio for free. That should be enough to test it out for your videos.

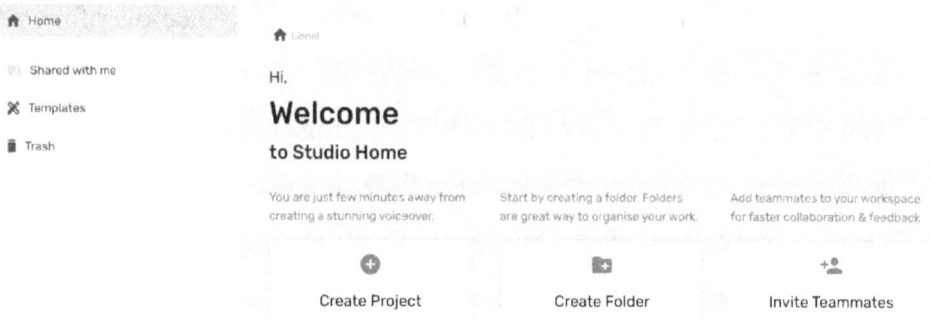

Once your in the dashboard, you can create a new project, a new folder or invite others to work on the project with you. I created a new folder named Murf Test.

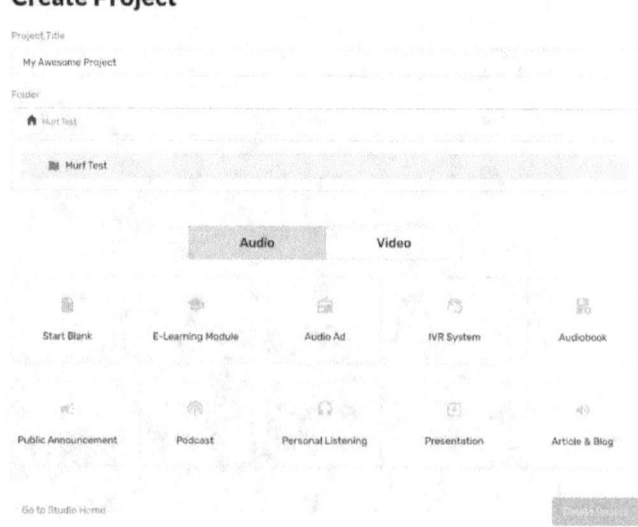

I then selected Video, and then clicked the Social Media icon. Once you are in the main work dashboard, you can start selecting the parts you need to work on. The next thing I did was go back to ChatGPT (or Jasper) and copied the text from the electric bike promo. I pasted it in the script box and then sifted through the many different voices to find the one that fits the best. You can also choose the tone that you want to use. I chose Promo since this will be a video highlighting the benefits of electric bikes.

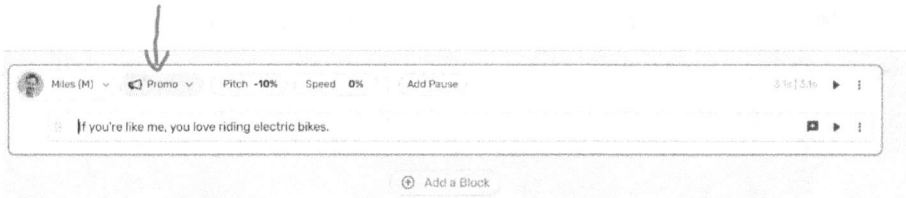

This is a bonus of Murf AI, since we might want different intonations depending on the video subject matter. You can also search for the voice you want based on country accent, age, and gender.

If the platform isn't saying the word you want correctly, you can add a pronunciation by either scrolling and highlighting the word or double clicking it. The pronunciation box will pop open.

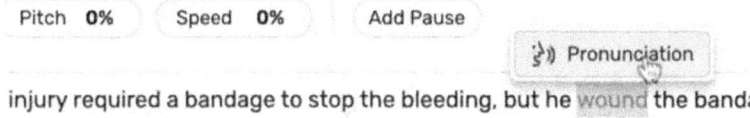

One of the good things about using Murf is that you can add the International Phonetic Alphabet (IPA) representation of a word. Since we didn't graduate in speech pathology (or did we), use ChatGPT to ask for the IPA of the word. The IPA of ChatGPT is tʃæt dʒiː piː tiː. Just copy and paste it in the IPA box, click preview and the word should be pronounced correctly.

Now, I'm making a simple one-line sentence to test out the platform with the electric bike example. I am using the line "If you're like me, you love riding electric bikes." I'm using the male Miles (US) voice. Since I want to add video to the project, I went down to the timeline and clicked the + icon next to the video icon.

I clicked the play button in the middle to preview the video and audio together.

The audio and the video sync perfectly, and I like the way it sounds. Murf can be a good alternative if you aren't happy with the stock voices on the video AI platforms. You can also add blocks to the timeline, which is useful if you're making longer pieces that need breaks and pauses. You can also add stock audio, and filter through genres such as mood, energy, and even instrument. There are also filters to help you find music for genres such as real estate and podcasting. You can use this to add background music to your videos.

Murf AI can also be used to make videos similar to the other platforms we used, but there is more emphasis on voice and more control and quality. They have lots of stock videos and images you can use for your videos. Also, it is a great platform to use for audiobooks or narration since the tone, quality, pitch, and speed can be adjusted. This can help in creating more inflections and nuances for storytelling. Just make sure the platform you sell on accepts AI voices.

If you are more audio focused, then Murf AI is an excellent choice, and will help you make amazing videos in a short amount of time.

Lovo AI

Lovo.AI is another high-quality audio AI platform. Their application is abundant with quality voices, and they have 100 languages with over 400 voices. I like Lovo because they have different AI tools to use. In addition to voices, they have an AI writer similar to Jasper and ChatGPT, art generation, voice cloning, and an online editor. Let's try out the platform. First, go to **lovo.ai** and sign-up for free. Most likely they will have a 2-week free trial available, which is one of the longer free trials out of all the AI tools we use. Then create a new project. This will take you to the main workspace and where you will do the bulk of the work.

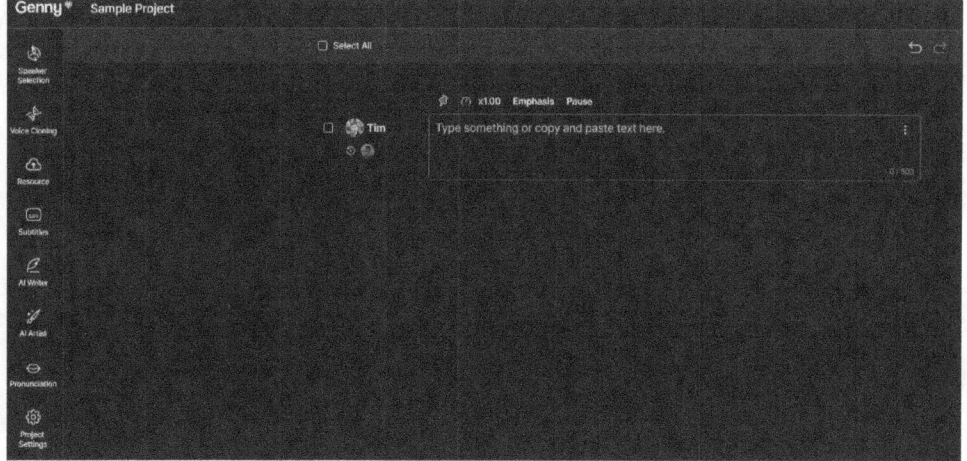

Lovo is built on a Deep Neural Network (DNN) platform and is powered by an AI model called Genny, which is their trademarked AI model.

The first thing I did was to go to the left-hand bar and selected AI writer.

The AI writer will work similar to other chatbots, where it will create text based off of prompts. When you click on the icon, the menu will pop open. Here you can select what type of content you want to make. This will tell the algorithm how it should present the responses it gives to you. I really like that there is a YouTube video option, since the bulk of my video content is for YouTube.

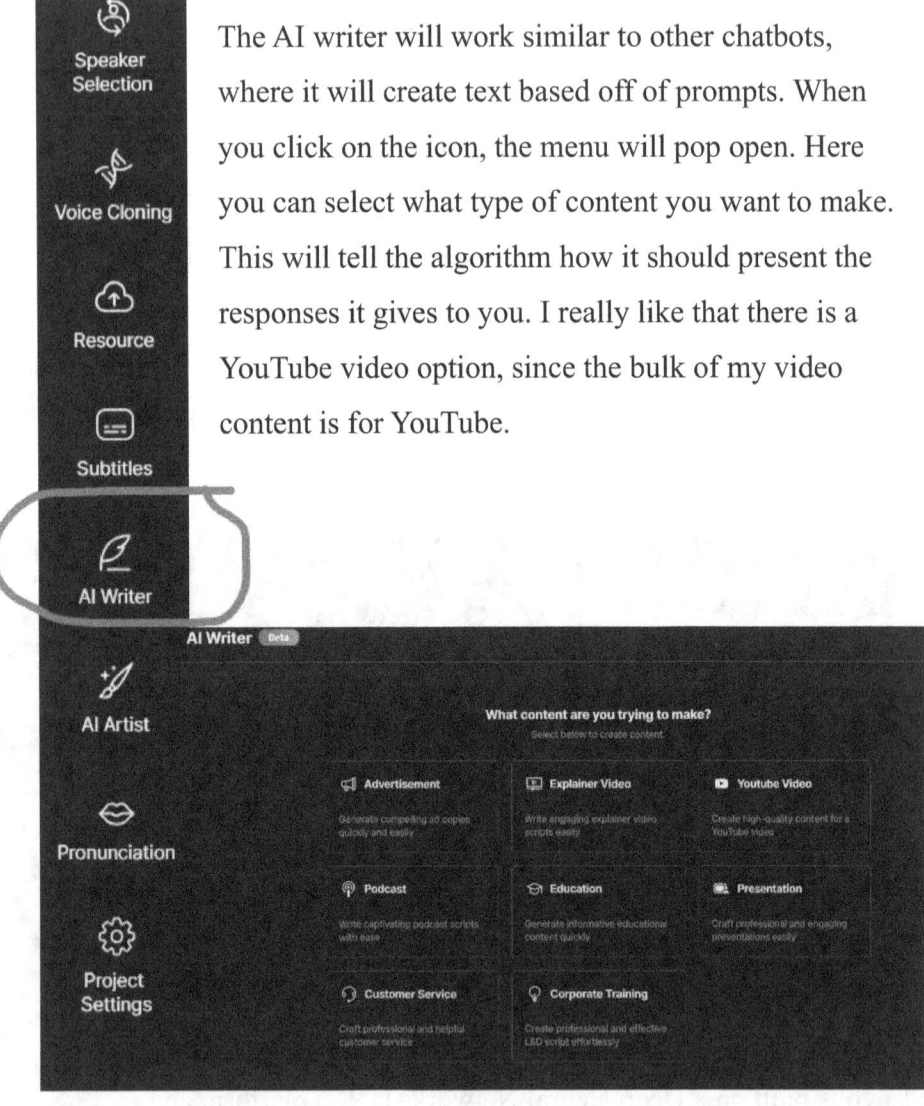

Next, you will fill out a few specific questions that will help to customize your videos.

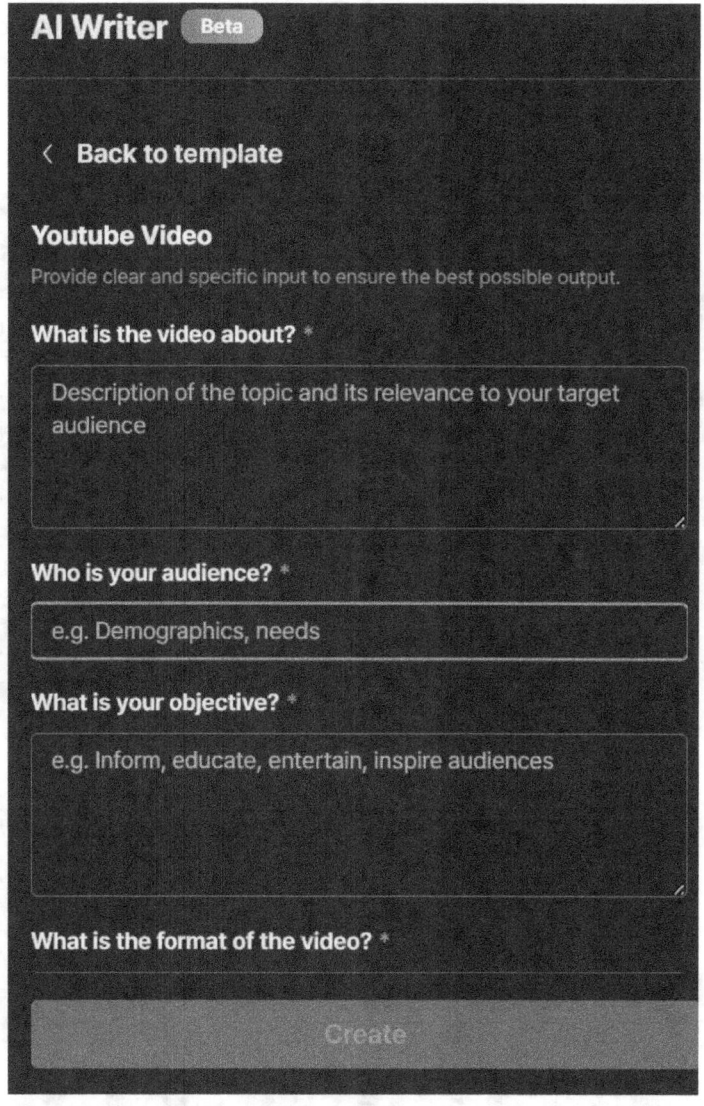

What I like about Lovo is that you can enter the specifications of the video, such as the objective of the video, the audience you're trying to reach, and a description of the video's topic. **You can even choose the tone and length you want the video to be.** After a minute, I had a complete YouTube video script, complete with transition cues, music spots, and where to insert video and images.

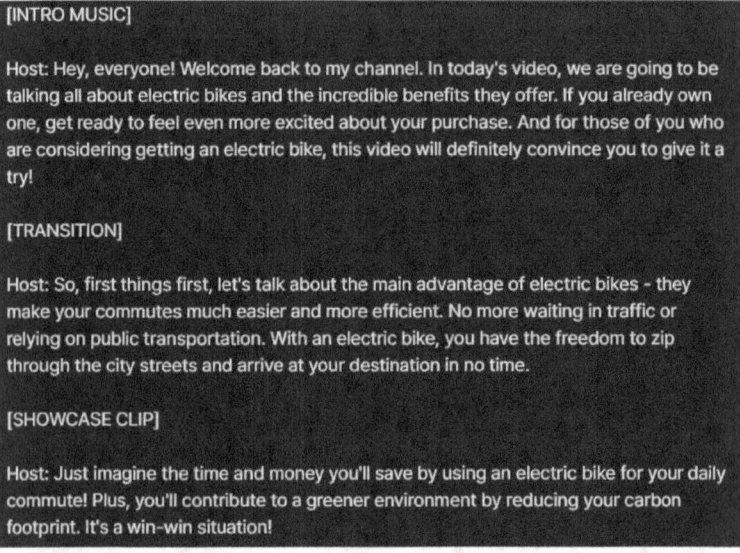

If you're not happy with the results, you can regenerate a new script, and you can even ask the AI writer to lengthen or shorten the script.

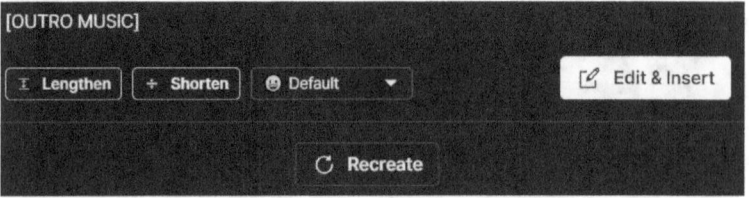

When you are happy with the results, add the text to the project. You will then be in the main dashboard again. Now you can select the voice you want to use by clicking on the voice name.

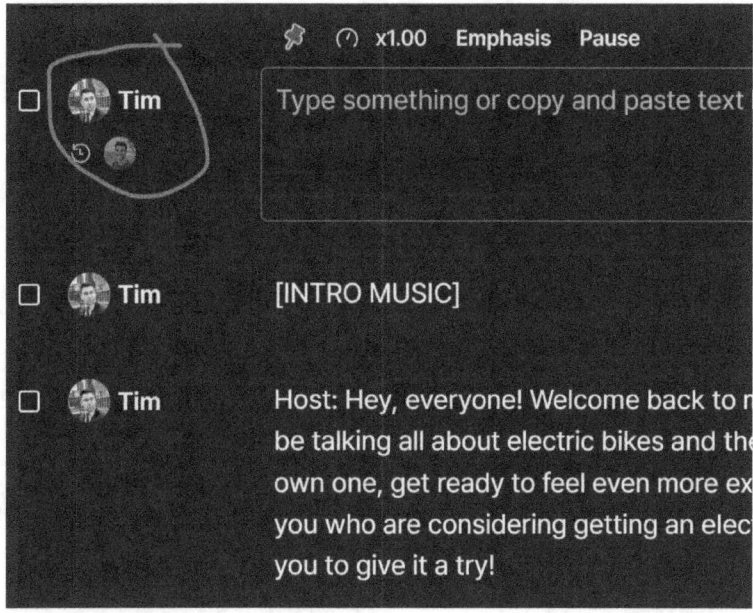

You can select from the numerous voices available. They have voices that are specific to audiobooks and narration. These voices have the resonance that you typically hear in car commercials and major advertising. There is even an option to use Global, which will have voices from around the world. This is good if you are going to place your ad or content in multiple countries. There are even Goblin voices, which is good if you are making animations or fiction audiobooks.

Once you found the voice you like, you can apply it to one or all text blocks, or you can have different voices for different blocks. After that, click the Generate button to have the voice sync with the text.

I chose the Tim voice, which sounded good for a product description video. After previewing it, I really like how it turned out. I then went to the left-side bar and selected Subtitles. I selected automatic subtitles to have the captions automatically generate and appear on the screen. If you ever notice YouTube ads, they usually have captions just in case the viewer has the sound off, they can still get their message across. I then headed over to AI Arist to create an image. I wanted to test this platform out rather than using the other applications.

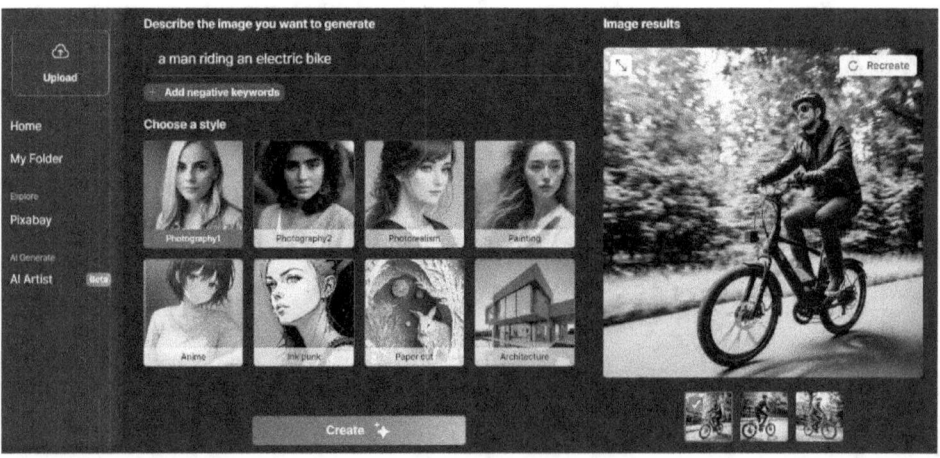

I used the prompt "a man riding an electric bike" and chose the Photography style and received three results in a matter of seconds. You can see the images are very realistic and lifelike. When you create images in AI Artists, they are stored in your personal folder. The free plan includes 1GB of storage that you can use, which will include any files that you upload outside of the platform. The one con of AI Artist is that you can't select all the images and add them into your project. You can only add one, then go back to generate again. They will be stored in your folder so you can use them later. Hopefully, this can be fixed in a future update.

If you don't like the images AI Artist creates (there's no reason not to) you can use free Pixabay stock images. There are plenty of images to choose from in pretty much every category. The integration of Pixabay inside Lovo is useful, and you can even use stock video and audio. There weren't too many videos on electric bikes here, but if you belong to Envato, you can download plenty and upload them in Lovo.

The other setting we will check on is the Project Settings tab. Here, you will be able to select the aspect ratio. This is important because you should customize the aspect ratio size according to the platform you're going to upload to, including YouTube or Instagram.

Another option is voice cloning. Let's say that you like your voice and have used it for other videos or voice-overs. You can upload voice samples of yourself speaking, and have AI make a cloned voice based off your tone and intonation. This is a good option if you've already established your voice on social media and want to make a lot of videos but don't have the time to record them all. You can input your script and have the AI make the videos for you without worrying about recording and editing.

The video turned out great. The audio is natural, realistic, and has proper modulation.

Hey, everyone! Welcome back to my channel. In today's video, we are going to be talking all about electric bikes

Out of all the AI platforms we explored, I think Lovo has one of the easier to use interfaces. It's clean, and there are only a handful of tools to use at once, so you don't get overwhelmed with a crowded UI.

We can use Lovo similarly to Murf and Pictory. We can make ads, blog post videos, and narration videos. I think Lovo is more natural than other AI voices, so it would be suited to more creative projects.

Another way we can make money with this platform is through YouTube ads. YouTube ads are relatively low-cost, and you can get thousands of views for a few hundred dollars. **The average Cost Per Click (CPC) of YouTube ads is $.10cents.** This means that you can get about 500 views to your video for around $50. The average click-through rate (CTR) for YouTube ads is 0.65%. This means that for every 1,000 impressions, an ad will receive an average of 6.5 clicks. Impressions mean how many times the ad shows, but not necessarily clicked. Depending on the type of ad you have, YouTube will only charge if the ad is clicked, or the video is played over a certain about of time and not skipped.

Let's say you want to do affiliate marketing. You are using an affiliate marketplace such as Clickbank or Share-a-Sale. You can use Lovo to promote your product. For example, you are promoting a meditation program. I did a Google search and found that women are more likely to meditate than men.

> Women were more likely to meditate than men, the CDC researchers found. Among adults surveyed in 2017, 16.3% of women said they had practiced meditation in the last year, compared with 11.8% of men. (There was no such gender gap among children, with 6% of girls and 4.9% of boys trying it at least once.) Nov 8, 2018

This can mean we should market our videos more towards females. In Lovo, select a female voice that is calming, then go to the AI writer and select advertisement, then in the demographics section write "women

18+." Write "I am selling a meditation program" for the <u>product or service</u> section, and "Generate clicks and views" for the <u>objective</u>. The AI writer wrote a nice script. Here is a sample:

"Introducing a Life-Changing Meditation Program just for you! Are you feeling overwhelmed by the stresses of everyday life? Do you yearn for a moment of deep relaxation and inner peace? Look no further! Our meditation program is here to provide you with the ultimate journey to tranquility. Designed exclusively for women like you, aged 18-65, our program is tailored to meet your specific needs and help you discover the power of mindfulness. Imagine a life where your worries melt away, leaving only a sense of calm and serenity. With our meditation program, that dream can become your reality."

It has some good points and is persuasive. You can customize the script by editing out what you don't want. When you have a specific program to promote, you can add that to the description box to have the AI Writer incorporate that data into the script. Experiment with the tone as well because it will change the overall mood of the script.

After this, go into AI Artist and generate a few "woman meditating" images, and select a few meditation videos. Add them to the project timeline and edit them together so you have a strong intro both visually and auditorily. Once you're happy with the video, you can promote your product by using YouTube ads. Let's use ClickBank as an example. If you haven't visited it before, ClickBank is a major affiliate marketplace. Businesses list products in the **Affiliate Marketplace** and marketers promote their products for a commission of the sales. Most likely, a landing page for the product will already be made, so all you have to do is market the product and get people to click the link to reach the product page. They will then need to purchase the product before you can earn a commission. This is easier said than done, but if you can create exciting video ads and get them in front of the right people, you should start to get clicks and views.

If you use ClickBank, you can sort through a vast number of products. You can then filter to find the highest converting products by selecting Gravity at the top-right corner.

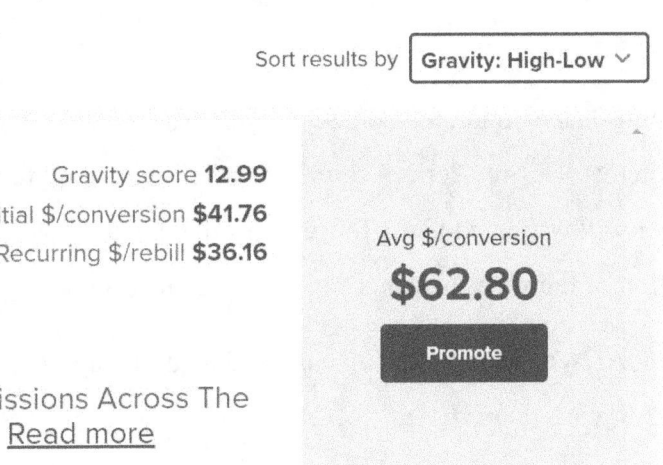

You can see this meditation product has an average conversion rate of $62.80 per sale, plus/or a recurring commission to the promoter.

I then went to the sell page and copied most of the text.

> InnaPeace™ is a series of CD-quality audio tracks with soothing sounds of nature and pleasant tones for relaxation and meditation.
>
> Embedded within each progressively deeper track are multiple proven Brainwave Guidance (BWG) technologies. These BWG components are virtually inaudible to the ear, yet harmlessly absorbed by the brain.
>
> Each deeper InnaPeace™ track also includes comprehensive support material, a document which explains how to achieve the maximum benefits from this breakthrough brainwave guidance technology and what to expect at each stage.
>
> The brainwave guidance technology (3xPureTone™) built into InnaPeace™ is so cutting-edge, it's unlike anything else in many respects.
>
> Now here's an illustration of **the brain before and after using InnaPeace™ brainwave guidance technology**. It shows the process of synchronising the brain's activity into alignment toward whole-brain-thinking:

I then went to Jasper, and created new content based on the AIDA (Attention, Interest, Desire, Action) framework. This is a good template because Jasper will write text using those four pillars, which will help get the attention of the viewer. Jasper made this great script:

"**Attention**: Are you looking for an easy and natural way to relax and meditate?

Interest: Introducing InnaPeace™ – a series of MP3-quality audio tracks with soothing sounds of nature and pleasant tones that can help take your relaxation and meditation to the next level. Our cutting edge brainwave guidance technology (3xPureTone™) embeds multiple proven BWG technologies in each track, which are virtually inaudible but harmlessly absorbed by your brain. Plus, every audio track contains comprehensive support material so you know exactly how to maximize its benefits.

Desire: Imagine what it would feel like if you could start feeling more relaxed, focused, positive and energized! With our unique program, you'll be able to strengthen and develop your brain similar to starting an exercise program - starting slow then building up intensity step by step until reaching deeper states of meditation.

Action: Experience InnaPeace™ today – sign up now and purchase one of our programs!

We can see that Jasper wrote a powerful ad script that we can use in our ads. You can see the first line "Are you looking for an easy and natural way to relax and meditate?" is the attention line. We have to captivate the viewer with the first 5 seconds. If I were searching on YouTube for meditation videos, then this ad popped up, most likely I would continue watching it. If it still looked good and had something I was looking for, I would click the ad, and if the product was something I needed, I would buy it. That's the basic flowchart of this type of digital marketing.

But what about the visuals? Good question. I went to Midjourney and created a woman meditating in photorealistic quality.

I then went to HeyGen and uploaded this image to the Talking Avatar section. I copied the script from Jasper, then pasted it in the avatar section.

I selected a voice that sounded like it would be good for an ad, then clicked Generate. After a few minutes, I had a nice one-minute video I can use for my ads or social media posts. A video like this should do well on TikTok. Just add your choice of background music and captions, and you should see the views start to generate.

I went into my Google Ads account and added 5 meditation keywords to the Forecast Planner. Meditation is a popular subject and has over 1million Google searches per month. Based on an average commission of $68, my ad could receive 360,000 impressions, 4,000 clicks, 68 conversions, and net a little over $4,000 a month.

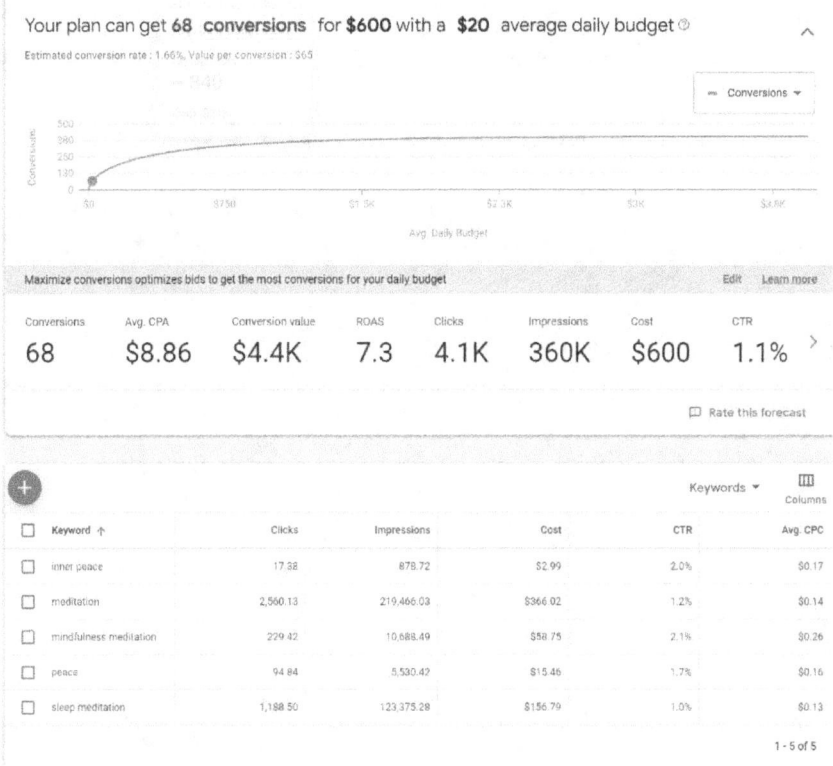

This is with an average Cost Per Click of $.15 cents. With my HeyGen video getting tens of thousands of impressions a day, it will also create a sense memory in viewer's head of meditation, which will then trigger when they see the ad again. It sometimes takes a few plays before a viewer will click an ad, but if they are ultimately interested in the subject matter, they should eventually make that click.

If you don't want to use HeyGen, you can use Lovo to make the videos and use their AI Artist to generate meditation images or use their Pixabay stock content to make the video. If the HeyGen, Lovo, or other video turned out to your satisfaction, you can run YouTube ads with that video.

Weekly estimates

👥 Available impressions ⌃

Based on your campaign settings but not your budget or bid

Impressions

81M

〜 Your estimated performance

Based on your targeting, settings, daily budget of $10.00 and bid of $0.06

Views	Impressions
2.8K – 6K	2.9K – 7.4K

Average CPV	Budget spend
$0.01 – $0.04	95% – 100%

Based on the keywords we made earlier, your ad could be viewed between 3,000 to 6,000 times per week with a median Cost Per View of $0.04 cents. If we increased the budget to $20 a day, we could get an estimated 5,500 to 12,000 views per week. This goes to show how important it is to have high-quality, captivating video.

But let's not forget about audio. Google has audio ads as well. Have you ever listened to a podcast and heard an ad suddenly play. That could've been a YouTube audio ad. These ads play on music and podcast channels and are often overlooked in favor of video. But with millions of daily listeners, you could miss out on sales if not utilizing this method.

Based on the same meditation keywords, my audio ad has the following stats:

  👥 **Available impressions**   ⌄
     1.1M impressions

  📈 **Your estimated performance**

Based on your targeting, settings, daily budget of $10.00 and bid of $4.51

Impressions	Average CPM
22K – 55K	$1.20 – $3.30

Budget spend	Unique reach
95% – 100%	11K – 30K

For a $10 a day campaign running for one month, I could get up to 30,000 unique impressions (how many times the ad was heard by a single user) per week. If 2% were to head over to our site from the ad, that's 2,400 people. If 10% purchased the meditation product at $68 commission, that's over $16,000 in gross pay from one audio ad.

These were just samples, but it shows the power of using AI in marketing. This is another reason AI audio tools like Lovo are so important in making excellent income these days. Lovo has natural, realistic voices that will not drive off a listener because it sounds too robotic like some other AI voices. It should do the opposite and engage them, making the listener feel comfortable and wanting to listen to more. Years ago, we would've needed to use voice-over artists and incur more expenses, driving down our profits, but now we can use AI tools to help build our generational wealth.

Conclusion

We looked at a lot of different AI tools that can give you a good starting point to make a lot of money by just using a computer. It can give you the freedom to make an income, but not keep you stuck in one place. I recently took a trip to Mexico and broke even on the travel costs because I took my laptop and was able to complete some work and get paid for it. Out of 8 days, I spent 5 hours working and had a pretty much free trip thanks to AI tools and knowledge.

Also, I like living by the rules of 5. Create 5 income sources, that make a minimum of $5,000 each per month. Once you make the first $1,000 in a month, to reach $5,000 will be easier since you will know the system that earned you your first $1K. Once you have acquired that stream, move onto the next. If you can make $5K on Amazon, $5K on YouTube, $5K on Shopify, etc. then you don't have to worry about losing one or even two streams since you will have the other three. To start, strive to earn $1,000 in one revenue stream before moving onto the others, but the goal should still be to reach $5,000 a month. This will all depend on how you well you learn and utilize AI tools with marketing efforts.

I can spend 200 pages writing about marketing and still not cover everything. Some key points to remember are to always make the first 5 seconds of your YouTube video the strongest. After that, viewers have the option to click "Skip Ad." Also, show your ad to the demographic of the product you're promoting. You wouldn't necessarily want to promote a hearing aid ad on an alternative rock channel. Also, make sure the product is good quality. If you are good at marketing and get a lot of people to view your ad and make sales, you might not make any money if there are a lot of returns. Do some research on the product, check similarweb.com to find the number of monthly visits and bounce rate, and maybe even order the product yourself to try it out. If you combine a great ad with a great product, you will most likely be successful in your marketing. Some of the top affiliate marketers make hundreds of thousands of dollars a year, and some are in the millions.

As of this writing, OpenAI has applied for a trademark for the next generation of the ChatGPT model, ChatGPT-5. No one can tell what the next incarnation will be, but one thing is for sure, ChatGPT and other AI tools are here to stay. They will get better and better as time goes on. It's up to you to put in the effort to learn the systems. Master one, then go on to the next. There is no guarantee that you will make money by using any of the tools in this book or anywhere else, but if you learn how to use them efficiently and effectively, you are much more likely to become significantly wealthy than if you don't learn them.

Bonuses!

Thank you for reading this book. I hope you enjoyed it and learned a lot. I used extensive research to find the best possible tools to help you make money with AI. In addition to this book, I have a YouTube channel called ROI Boost. You might find some more helpful information there. Scan the QR code to go to the channel.

If you found this book useful, please leave an honest review on Amazon. This will help to shape future incarnations of the book, since I will update it as future tools and updates become available.

Also, I have 1,000 FREE ChatGPT prompts for you to use. Each is categorized in their own niche. Here is an example for YouTube:

What are some strategies for promoting/building/engaging my YouTube channel's email list/newsletter/community and cultivating/nurturing/growing subscribers? You will just need to select the best option for your case.

Head over to myroiboost.com/bonus

Honorable Mentions

I regularly use all the tools listed in this book for my online businesses and have found them all very useful. However, I tried many others, but do not use them often, but you may find them helpful. Here are other AI tools to use in business.

DALL-E 2 (PROS) Is an AI image generation platform. It can create realistic images based on text prompts. (CONS) No free trial or free credits.

Neural.love (PROS) Free AI image generator that produces excellent results. (CONS) Mostly good for cartoonish images. No direct editing.

Runway AI (PROS) Text to Video application that can generate video based off text prompts. Also, you get free credits. (CONS) Video quality is often low, and it could take several prompts to get a decent generation.

Synthesys Studio (PROS) AI video, audio, and image creator. Can make AI videos of long-length, and images of decent quality. (CONS) No trial or free credits. Will need to purchase separate plans to use AI Voice with AI Video.

Designs.ai (PROS) Can create logos, scripts, videos, and voice-overs. You can make mockups for free to try out the platform. (CONS) Limited number of templates as of this writing.

Tips & Tricks

We learned a lot about using AI tools in this book, but there is still a lot to learn. Key points to remember are: do not get overwhelmed, fulfill one project before starting another, don't neglect social media.

Some more key points to remember.

1. Build a bulk of social media and schedule it to post throughout the month. If you make 30 days' worth of content in two days, you will have the next two days to make another 30 days of content for another project...and so on. I usually spend the first weekend of the month making the following months YouTube content. This way, I can focus on other things throughout the rest of the month. Do this for all your social media, and you can edit later if you think of something you want to add.

2. Some say blogs are a thing of the past, but if you search for pretty much anything these days, there will be a blog review or comparison or product guide of a product. Do a Google search for iPhone 14 and after the major phone brands, there will be lots of blog reviews, many you probably never heard of. Copy the link and search similarweb.com. I bet the majority of the blogs have at least 200,000 visitors a month. Considering they most likely have affiliate links and AdSense turned on, they very well might be making thousands of dollars a month just by posting in their blogs. We now have AI tools to

make the process faster, simpler, and prettier. Some blogs have bad designs, but we can now make our blogs look like those of the future.

3. Stick it out. I have personally taught friends and others about e-commerce, dropshipping, YouTube, etc. and they did it for a couple months, didn't make much money, then quit. You don't be like them. If someone told you in two years you could make $150,000 a year just by posting on YouTube and social media, but you have to post multiple times a week and be consistent…would you do it? You will most likely need to pay rent in 2 years, so why would you give up after a couple of months? If you could make half that in 1 year, would you do it then? The people who make over six-figures online stay persistent. They keep at it and don't give up. This is a long-term game. If you consistently post high-quality content month after month, you will most likely see an increase in views and visits every single month. If you take nothing else from this book, it is to be CONSISTANT.

Disclaimer:

The advice stated in this book does not constitute it will work with everyone. Earning money online takes dedication, work, and training. The information provided in this book is for general informational purposes only. The authors and publishers of this book are not engaged in rendering legal, financial, or professional advice. While we have made every effort to ensure the accuracy and completeness of the information presented, we cannot guarantee that the content is up-to-date, error-free, or applicable to your specific circumstances. If you require expert assistance in any area, including but not limited to business, finance, law, or any other field, we strongly recommend that you consult with a qualified professional who can provide tailored advice based on your individual situation. The authors and publishers disclaim any and all liability to any person or entity for any loss, damage, or inconvenience caused or alleged to be caused directly or indirectly as a result of the use, application, or interpretation of the information presented in this book. The views expressed by the authors are their own and do not necessarily represent the views of any organizations they may be affiliated with. Reading this book implies your acceptance of this disclaimer. If you do not agree with the terms outlined in this disclaimer, you should not use this book or its contents. Always conduct your own research, seek professional advice, and use your best judgment before making any business decisions.

Affiliate Disclaimer:

Some of the links in this book may be affiliate links, which means that the author and publisher may earn a commission if you click on the link and make a purchase. This comes at no additional cost to you.

The author and publisher only recommend products or services that they believe may be of value to readers. However, the decision to purchase through affiliate links is entirely voluntary and solely at the discretion of the reader.

The author and publisher are not responsible for the quality, accuracy, timeliness, reliability, or any other aspect of the products or services offered by third-party vendors or affiliates. Any issues or concerns regarding products or services purchased through affiliate links should be directed to the respective vendor.

The use of affiliate links helps to support the author and publisher in providing free and valuable content to readers. Your support is greatly appreciated.

www.ingramcontent.com/pod-product-compliance
Lightning Source LLC
Chambersburg PA
CBHW070010300526
45794CB00001B/268